LORDS ❖ OF ❖ MAGIC™

PRIMA'S OFFICIAL STRATEGY GUIDE

Joe Grant Bell

Prima Publishing
Rocklin, California
(916) 632-4400
www.primagames.com

CONTENTS

Introduction V

CHAPTER 1: EARLY DECISIONS 1
Character Class 2
Game Difficulty 11
The Impact of Your Choices 14

CHAPTER 2: BLUEPRINTS FOR SUCCESS 15
Starting Out 16
Empire Building 29
Late-Game Techniques 36
Taking Over More Faiths 40
Onward to Battle! 41

CHAPTER 3: THE INNER WORKINGS OF URAK 43
Terrain 44
Important Structures .46
Upgrades 54
Unit Types 55
Experience 58
Fame 60
Intelligence and Barter 61
Thief Activities 65
Magic and Combat 66

CHAPTER 4: COMBAT 67
When to Fight 67
Building Armies 69
Overview of Combat .72
Combat Subtleties 77
Final Combat Notes 83

CHAPTER 5: MAGIC 85
Air Spells 86
Chaos Spells 96
Death Spells 106
Earth Spells 117
Fire Spells 125
Life Spells 134
Order Spells 143
Water Spells 152

CHAPTER 6: EMPIRE BUILDING 163
Initial Troubles: Tips for the Early Game 164
Mid-Game Tips 167
Late-Game Tips 172
Unit Comparisions 175
Fighting Balkoth 183

CHAPTER 7: COMBAT UNITS OF URAK 189
Air Units 192
Chaos Units 202
Death Units 212
Earth Units 223
Fire Units 233
Life Units 243
Order Units 253
Water Units 263

CHAPTER 8: ARTIFACTS 273
Greater Artifacts 274
Lesser Artifacts 284
Usage Charts 305

INTRODUCTION

Lords of Magic is, among other things, a game of vast possibilities. With eight faiths and three character classes to choose from—not to mention countless spells, artifacts, and units to research, collect, and do battle with—you can bet that it'll be a long time before you see every combination that Urak has to offer. This remarkable variety can be exhilarating, but it can also leave you feeling a little lost. This book is designed to help you get past the initial confusion, get a grip on the game world, and master its countless options.

Since **Lords of Magic** is an open-ended experience where the outcome is never certain, you will find that the majority of this book is not devoted to precise formulas for winning. Instead, the book is filled with pages upon pages of factual information on spells, artifacts, and units that exist in the world of Urak. This knowledge will help you understand what's going on behind the scenes and will allow you to develop your own personal strategies.

This book also serves as a reference text. Whether you want to find out which faith owns the spell Heroic Demise, how many Hit Points a Storm Lord possesses, or exactly how powerful Balkoth's Scythe is, you've come to the right place.

This book is organized into eight chapters. They are as follows:

- Chapter 1 is an introduction to the game's faiths and character classes.

- Chapter 2 provides a blueprint for early success, explaining the flow of a typical **Lords of Magic** game in general terms.

- Chapter 3 covers some of the subtler points of Urak.

- Chapter 4 reviews the art of combat.

- Chapter 5 is a roster of every spell in the game, complete with casting costs and notes.

- Chapter 6 contains game tips for the advanced player.
- Chapter 7 provides hard numerical statistics on every unit in the game.
- Chapter 8 is a roster of every artifact in Urak, including notes on artifact powers.

Urak is a land of variety, and with the help of this book, you'll soon master this variety rather than let it bewilder you. You have taken the first steps toward becoming a true Lord of Magic....

ACKNOWLEDGMENTS

Thanks to the following people for their help with this book:

Paul Bushland for creating numerous charts and tables,

Glenn Oliver for providing much of the information that went into this book, and

Richard Dal Porto for putting it all together.

CHAPTER

1

EARLY DECISIONS

Every game of **Lords of Magic** poses similar challenges: you must recapture your faith's Great Temple, build your Stronghold, assimilate other faiths, and eventually challenge Balkoth for supremacy in Urak. Every time you play, however, there will be major differences in how events take place. These differences—subtle or blatant—are often triggered in part by your choice of Lord, faith, and level of game difficulty.

This chapter examines the choices you must make before the game even starts. It begins with an examination of character class, followed by in-depth summaries of the game's eight faiths. The chapter ends with a look at game difficulty and how it will affect your strategy.

CHARACTER CLASS

Your first decision in **Lords of Magic** is to select a character class for your Lord. The Lord, the leader of your faith, is the only character that can attain the twelfth level. Regular Champions can only reach the tenth level.

You may decide between three character classes: Warrior, Mage, or Thief. Your decision will impact the game in several areas; it's important to choose carefully instead of leaping right in. To some degree, you're committing yourself to a certain style of play when you pick a character. This section explains the ramifications of playing each character type.

THE SIGNIFICANCE OF CHARACTER CLASS

It's important to know what you're choosing when you pick a character class. You aren't choosing a class for your whole faith—you're just picking a class for your leader. There's nothing that says your Mage Lord can't hire lots of Warrior Champions or that your Thief Champion can't hire lots of Mages. On the surface, your Lord's character class may seem almost trivial. How much difference can a single unit make?

As you start to play, however, you'll realize that this decision carries considerable weight. Your Lord will be your most powerful unit throughout much of the game—perhaps through the **entire** game. Also, consider that various actions require high-level characters of a particular type; effective spellcasting, for example, requires a skilled Mage. Advanced Thief actions, such as stealing and taking prisoners, are also quite difficult unless you have a high-level Thief on your side. Therefore, if you're intent on casting spells, sneaking around, or capturing the enemy, you'll be giving yourself a boost by selecting a Mage or Thief right away.

You'll find yourself locked into certain paths depending on what type of Lord you select. If you choose a Mage, you must devote some time to spell research; otherwise, your Lord won't be particularly lordly in battle.

On the other hand, if you pick a Warrior, you can skip the research, for the most part, and get right down to combat.

WARRIOR

The Warrior is, by far, the easiest character class to play. Warriors aren't necessarily any more powerful than Mages or Thieves, but they're so straightforward that you won't have to worry about subtle details when you play them. The Warrior's best strategy is to bash the enemy with big armies of veteran troops, largely ignoring the niceties of spellcasting and thievery.

It's possible to hire Mages and pursue spell research even if you have a Warrior Lord—it just isn't as **efficient** as it would be with a Mage Lord. In the early stages of the game, your Lord is destined to be involved in most every combat you take part in, just because your other troops aren't powerful enough and need their Lord's help. If your Lord happens to be a Mage, this results in a high-level spellcaster who can engage in fast spell research and cast multiple spells in battle. If your Lord is a Warrior or Thief, however, you'll have to go somewhat out of your way to engage in serious spellcasting.

Warriors can rally their troops during combat, resulting in fractional increases in combat abilities. These fractions do add up, especially in close battles. This ability to rally augments the Warrior's innate combat ability.

If your Warrior decides to avoid thievery and spellcasting altogether, it's vital to explore and gain experience points. During the game's **early** stages, brute strength tends to rule, but Mages and Thieves can get the upper hand as they research potent spells and hone their thieving skills, respectively.

The main risk with Warrior Lords is the temptation to have them fight **too** much; your game ends if your Lord is killed without a successor. Despite your Warrior Lord's combat prowess, he can't stand alone. You must keep a close watch on his Hit Points at all times during battle. Have him be a spectator instead of a participant when his health starts to slip.

> When you send your Warrior Lord into battle, be sure that he's supported with other melee units. This way he won't draw all the attention. If you send your Lord to battle the enemy alone, he'll be overwhelmed by sheer numbers. (See Chapter 4 for more information on combat).

MAGE

If your plans include spell research and spellcasting, a Mage Lord is an excellent choice. Your Mage Lord's high level will contribute greatly to your research efforts and will provide a conduit for that research once it's completed.

Mages are a little harder to use, but can help your war effort if used creatively. As they gain power, however, they become more and more useful. Increased mana capacity allows them to cast spells over and over, while research provides new and powerful spells that can alter the face of battle. Potions of Mana are critical to early game play as it can double the amount of mana available to a Mage.

Your Mage Lord can and should tag along in early battles despite his fragility and lack of power—this is the only way of gaining experience. You must, however, think of the Mage as more of an onlooker than a participant. Keep him well away from enemies with long-range attacks. In this way, your Mage Lord will gain ability without taking undue risks.

Mage Lords require more decision-making than Warrior Lords. When should you have your Mage Lord stop fighting and start researching? What spells should you research? A good policy is to have the Mage Lord fight until you have entered a "consolidation" phase of your game, where you try to build up some defense for newly gained territory. At that point, your

Mage can start to engage in research, stopping only when he is needed in a particularly important battle.

THIEF

Thieves are an unusual choice for a Lord. If your Lord isn't a Thief, you might tend to use Thieves only as scouts and supplemental attackers, ignoring their unique abilities altogether. At earlier levels, Thieves are effective as archers. At later levels, they're quite deadly. Remember that most Thief skills work best when the Thief's level is higher than that of the intended target he's trying to hide from, steal from, or interrogate.

If you happen to possess a Thief Lord, however, his special Thief skills will become second nature. Instead of attacking enemies, you'll learn to rob them first; instead of killing everyone in a party, you'll learn to Subdue Champions and interrogate them for useful information.

Just as a Mage Lord makes it much easier and more convenient for you to engage in intense spellcasting and research, a Thief Lord makes it easier for you to engage in Thief activities with a reasonable degree of success.

FAITH

Your choice of faith has a big impact on what sort of game you'll play. Here's a brief synopsis of each faith, complete with notes on their strengths and weaknesses. This list will help you select a faith that fits with your preferred style of play.

AIR

Air features strong Lords and Champions but relatively lackluster infantry and cavalry. This forces you to rely on missile troops, as Air's melee armies tend to lack the power to stand toe-to-toe with tough legions from Fire, Chaos, Earth, or Death.

> BOTTOM LINE: Chaos is a great faith for players who like to build crushing armies. Its conventional troops can defeat most other troops in the game. Chaos Mages need to be extremely patient and must look for ways to minimize the risk of their own potent, unpredictable spells.

DEATH

 Death is the only faith that cannot be played from the very start—you must defeat Balkoth at least once before the option to play Death becomes available. Selecting a Mage Lord when you play the Death faith allows you to play Balkoth himself.

Death is a potent faith, whose infantry and cavalry start out middle-of-the-road but, like its later spells, are truly devastating. Death's armies are generated largely with the help of Mages. Death is the only faith in the game that allows fairly powerful creatures to be summoned during combat and then to continue in the game world. The net result is ravening hordes of Skeletons and Death Shades.

The Death spell book contains a wide array of damaging spells and the aforementioned summoning spells.

Balkoth is a larger-than-life ruler; he's the main reason why Death is so formidable. Armed with his special Scythe and a ready supply of mana, he's capable of wrecking whole armies by himself.

Death starts the game in a loose alliance with Chaos, Earth, and Fire.

> BOTTOM LINE: Death's missile units are arguably the best in the game, but keep in mind that Death's units don't heal as quickly, and their undead units don't heal at all. More impressive are Death's spells and Balkoth himself. Balkoth's mere presence turns Death from a strong faith into a deadly powerhouse.

EARTH

Earth is a tough combat faith. At the core of its power are sturdy, stocky Dwarven infantry and fast cavalry. These units rank among the hardiest in the land and cause considerable damage with their attacks. Their only true drawback is their extreme sluggishness in overland travel and in the throes of combat.

Earth's spell book is filled with practical combat spells that enhance friendly units' combat skills. Another specialty is its ability to immobilize the enemy, whether in a limited sense (as with Slow) or dramatically (as with the powerful Turn to Stone).

Combat with Earth units is typically one-sided. If the Earth units manage to get close to the enemy fast enough, they do fairly well. Their slow speed, however, makes them vulnerable to spells and missiles hurled from afar.

Earth begins the game in a loose alliance with Chaos, Death, and Fire.

> **BOTTOM LINE:** Impatient players will lament Earth's sluggish movement. But if you like to muster grinding, bruising armies, you'll love Earth units' power and balanced offensive and defensive capabilities.

FIRE

Fire units are much like those of Chaos—heavy on offense, light on defense, and extremely deadly in packs. Fire units take this principle to an even greater height than Chaos units and feature the best all-around attack skills in the game. As a result, they can make mincemeat of just about anything.

Fire spells cause extreme damage and can be dangerous to both sides of a fight. Some Fire spells confer large benefits but also confer penalties; some spells damage the caster or other friendly units to achieve a powerful effect; and some spells damage every unit in combat, including ones on the caster's side. It takes some forethought and planning to make the most of Fire's spells because, like Chaos's spells, Fire's spells can hurt just as much as they can help.

Fire starts the game in a loose alliance with Chaos, Death, and Earth.

> **BOTTOM LINE: Fire is for those gameplayers who crave pure offense and could care less about defense. Fire units' great power easily crushes armies of equal or smaller size, but their poor defense ensures that they'll take serious losses in a battle with a potent foe.**

LIFE

 As a whole, Life is one of the most powerful faiths. Their missile troops are excellent, but their infantry and cavalry are usually defeated by equal-sized hordes from Earth, Fire, or Chaos. They're very fast, however; and, to some degree, this makes up for their fragility. Life units also tend to recover from wounds more quickly than other faiths' troops, which allows for a faster-paced game since there is less waiting around to heal.

Life magic emphasizes healing. This is an excellent feature, as healing allows a Life Lord to keep his troops alive despite their relative fragility. Veteran troops are Life's most important resources in the game; the benefits of healing should be immediately obvious.

Life units' speed makes it easy to get a quick start and to explore the map thoroughly.

Life starts the game in a loose alliance with Air, Order, and Water.

> **BOTTOM LINE:** Life offers fast units and strong healing powers. Effective use of healing and long-range attackers pave the way to victory, but a player who insists on building one-dimensional melee armies will have a difficult time playing Life.

ORDER

Of all the "good" faiths in Urak (Air, Life, Order, and Water), Order is the most militarily inclined. Its troops can't match the extreme power of Fire and Chaos, but they frequently come close. Order's units possess excellent defensive skills; its infantry, cavalry, and missile troops are all extremely competent.

Speed is a non-issue with Order; its troops usually rank among the middle echelons of mobility.

Order's spell book is also excellent. A wide range of spells that enhance combat skills are backed up by unique potent spells such as Possession, which allows the caster to take control of an enemy unit.

Order begins the game in a loose alliance with Air, Life, and Water.

> **BOTTOM LINE:** Order is a potent, versatile faith that's good for just about any strategy you may pursue. Bear in mind that Order is the "enforcer" of the good faiths in Urak. If you choose to play Order, you better do a good job—the other good faiths aren't as powerful and can't bail you out of trouble! Order is the strongest faith with the best fighters and the best spells.

WATER

Water troops are usually balanced and are seldom at the bottom of any statistical category—but they're seldom at the top. Its units' speed is quite good overall, and in fact, this is the one area where they actually stand out. Also, many Water units are capable of crossing watery areas without ships.

Water spells include a number of healing spells and several spells that confer both benefits and drawbacks. Many of these spells, however, can easily be combined with one another to minimize drawbacks.

Water begins the game in a loose alliance with Air, Order, and Life.

> **BOTTOM LINE:** Water is another faith that's good for any type of strategy. Water starts off in a good defensive position. It favors a mixture of melee and missile attacks, with magic in support and ships that can take trips wherever they need to go.

GAME DIFFICULTY

Game difficulty has a profound effect on your **Lords of Magic** experience. In a nutshell, here is what to expect from the different difficulty settings.

EASY

Easy games are indeed quite easy, especially once you've mastered the basics of **Lords of Magic.** In Easy games, you can expect the following:

- Extra resources for you and all "neutral" faiths at the game's beginning, which allow you to hire lots of mercenaries and take over caves easily.

- A Death faith that starts with fewer resources than its counterpart in harder games.

- Extra loot when you win battles.

- A big percentage of a faith's troops whenever that particular faith swears allegiance to you.

- Extra scrolls.

- The Great Temple is easier to conquer.

With a little practice, you should be able to blast through an Easy game in no time. Easy games tend to make a game's first few turns quite effortless, in stark contrast to the first few turns of Medium and Hard games. Easy games also give you extra time to build your empire, as Balkoth is less likely to show up as quickly as he is in the harder games.

It's not recommended that you play too many games on the Easy level, or you'll develop bad gameplaying habits. The Easy level doesn't force you to be efficient and, without that pressure, you probably won't be.

MEDIUM

Here's what to expect from Medium-difficulty games:

- Fairly limited initial resources for you and all "neutral" faiths.

- A Death faith that begins with less of a disadvantage than the one in an Easy game.

- A normal "default" amount of loot from victorious combats.

- A normal "default" number of free troops whenever a faith swears allegiance to you.

The Medium-difficulty level makes the game's first few turns fairly rough; you have to scramble to keep your army alive and build up sufficient strength to retake your Great Temple. Once you have retaken the Great Temple, the difficulty does smooth out a bit.

Balkoth sometimes shows up quite early in a Medium-difficulty game, though this is never a certainty. Medium difficulty forces you to strive for efficiency in every phase of the game.

Some players prefer a relaxing, low-key game that provides a good challenge without a truly vicious computer opponent. These players will be content to keep playing Medium-difficulty games long after their skills have surpassed it. Others will want to try a Hard game once they have mastered the Medium level.

HARD

Hard-difficulty games are a genuine challenge. Here's what to expect from them:

- Very limited starting resources for you and for the "neutral" faiths.

- Death receives an extra Champion at the game's beginning.

- Below-average loot from successful combat.

- A very small number of free troops when a faith swears allegiance to you.

- Fewer scrolls.

- The Great Temple is more difficult to conquer.

The Hard-difficulty level doesn't alter game mechanics in any hidden way; it simply produces the effects we just reviewed. That doesn't mean Hard difficulty is a cakewalk—these changes are significant. You'll have a very hard time taking over your Great Temple at the start of a Hard game, and Balkoth tends to have a jump on you—so watch out!

The Hard-difficulty level is best attempted after you have played and won a few games at Medium difficulty.

THE IMPACT OF YOUR CHOICES

You can select any combination of leader class and faith in the game and still succeed at any difficulty level. The point of this chapter wasn't to discourage you from choosing unusual combinations, but rather to let you know which classes and faiths excel in which areas. By choosing a class and faith best suited to the strategy you wish to employ, you can make the game much easier and more enjoyable.

The remainder of this book provides detailed strategies on how to win the game and raw information on game units and spells that will help you fuel those strategies.

CHAPTER

BLUEPRINTS FOR SUCCESS

This chapter is a quick guide to success in **Lords of Magic.** It won't teach you many subtle tricks, and it doesn't go into great detail on individual spells and units that help make your plans of conquest a reality. Rather, it provides you with a general overview of how to proceed in a typical **Lords of Magic** game, so that you'll have a solid foundation of knowledge during your first few visits to Urak.

Later chapters contain more detailed information on the game and how it works. Refer to these later chapters after you have spent some time with **Lords of Magic,** and they'll help you to improve your level of play even more.

STARTING OUT

After selecting a leader class and faith, you'll be plunked down unceremoniously in the harsh world of Urak. What can you expect to find there? What assets do you possess? And exactly what are your goals? The following pages will help you make sense of your first few turns.

WORLD STATE

Every game of **Lords of Magic** poses unexpected twists and turns. But there are certain constants you can count on every time you play. Here's a look at these constants and the benefits you can gain by understanding them.

THE MAP

Lords of Magic is played on fixed topographical maps. You can **either** choose to play on the default map by selecting New Game from the main menu **or** select Custom and choose to play on a map you have created with the Map Editor. (If you forgot what your custom map looks like, use the Map Editor to preview it.)

Each faith has a particular type of terrain associated with it. Fire, for example, starts the game in a territory featuring lava-covered plains. As you explore the map, it's easy to see where your faith's territory ends and another faith's territory begins—the terrain itself marks the border between two different faiths.

> Border towns are another sure-fire indicator that you're at the edge of your lands. You'll always find a border town between two adjacent faiths—they're NEVER found in the middle of one particular faith's territory.

Maps may initially seem to have many random elements, but this randomness is limited to structure placement. For example, your faith's Barracks won't always be in exactly the same place every time. During one game it may appear slightly north of your Capital, while in another game it appears to the south. There is a limit to this randomization, however. Your crucial outlying structures (Barracks, Mage Tower, Library, and Thieves' Guild) will always appear within one turn's march of your Capital. Other important structures, such as mines and caves, are also guaranteed to appear somewhere near each faith's Capital.

Fig. 2-1. Outlying structures, such as Barracks and Mage Towers, appear in random positions. Structures holding enemies (mines, caves, statues, etc.) also pop up in random spots.

While the placement of certain structures varies slightly from game to game, not everything is random. Capitals, Villages, and Great Temples are immune to randomization altogether and never budge an inch. Furthermore, the topography of the land itself doesn't change. If you see a mountain or lake at a certain point on a particular map, you're guaranteed to find it in the same spot the next time you play on that map.

Since Capitals and topography never change, you would be right to assume that the overall placement of faiths is similarly carved in stone. If you play on a given map and find that the Water faith starts in a certain locale, you can rest assured that Water will start in that same spot for **every** game played on that map. To put it another way, each map has a predetermined territory set aside for each faith, and that particular faith always starts

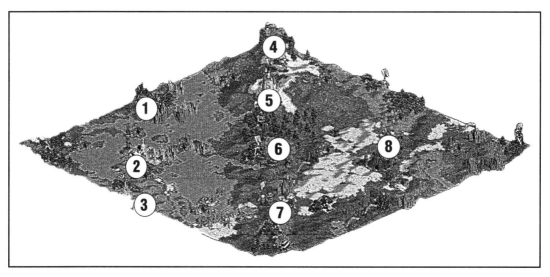

Fig. 2-2. This diagram illustrates where each faith's territory is located in relation to the other faiths.

Faiths' Capitals

1. Death   5. Air
2. Water   6. Order
3. Life   7. Earth
4. Chaos   8. Fire

the game in the appropriate territory. Figure 2-2 shows the relative positions of each faith's territory on the standard world map of Urak.

Note that figure 2-2 is a two-dimensional map representing a true 3D world without any edges—you need to imagine what this map would look like when wrapped around a sphere. For example, if your army traveled due west from the Death Capital, it wouldn't run into the "edge of the world." Instead, the army would pop up on the exact opposite side of figure 2-2 (south of the Fire Capital) and would continue west until it eventually reached the Earth Capital.

Figure 2-2 is helpful for determining which neighbors to expect. For example, when playing the Air faith, you can expect to find Chaos to the north, Order to the south, Life to the east, and Death to the west.

STRUCTURES

As noted earlier, structures are the only random element on the map. Barracks, Thieves' Guilds, Mages' Guilds, and Libraries are always very close to your Capital, even though their placement is somewhat random. Other structures, such as caves and dungeons, are a bit more random in their locations.

You can rest assured that the most readily available enemy structures will be caves; a number of them will appear within one day's walk of your Capital.

> As we'll see in Chapter 3, caves' names and appearances depend on the terrain they're found in. In Earth terrain, for example, caves are called Mushroom Patches, while in Water territory they're called Oceanic Shrines. In Fire territory, they're just called caves. Regardless of a cave's name and appearance, however, these structures all have the same function: they're common monster hideouts that serve you well when you're itching for a fight. Whenever we refer to caves in this book, we refer to this whole class of structures.

What effect does structure randomization have? For one thing, it ensures that exploration is always vital. You can't bet on any particular structure (save for Capitals, Villages, and Great Temples) being in any particular place; you will have to employ scouts to find out what's out there. Also, you can never be certain of any structure's "toughness." The farther away the cave is from your city, the stronger it is.

Fig. 2-3. Check the Stronghold's Intelligence Report to see how other faiths view you.

YOUR OPPONENTS

You'll face seven other faiths in each game of **Lords of Magic.** These faiths are not always at odds with you, however. Some faiths are friendly and represent a potential source of trade. It's important to keep tabs on your relations with other faiths by frequently checking the Intelligence Report in your Stronghold. (See figure 2-3.)

In the middle stages of the game, your main objective is to take over several of these other faiths. This expands your territories, provides new Strongholds to assign your loyal followers to, and opens up the possibility of buying units you haven't yet owned.

In addition to other faiths, you have to deal with Renegade parties. Renegades are nominally affiliated with a specific faith, but they're **not** its representatives. In other words, Renegades always are hostile—even though you may have good relations with their associated faith. Watch them carefully, or they'll ruin your outlying structures.

Finally, though Death is in some ways "just another faith," in other ways it **definitely** is not. Although you may have good relations with the Death faith in the early stages of any given game, you must bear in mind that Death's ultimate ambition is to crush all opposition—and that includes you. At some point, you can expect a head-on attack from Balkoth himself, and you better hope you're prepared when that time comes. The attack may come unexpectedly—for example, right after you have traded successfully with Balkoth or have offered him a gift!

YOUR ASSETS

You start the game with very little. In a typical Medium-difficulty scenario, you start with a Lord at the second or third level, a scouting unit, a missile unit, and one melee unit. Your gold, ale, and crystals are limited (30 of each resource at Easy difficulty, 18 of each at Medium difficulty, and 12 of each at Hard). It is absolutely vital to start conquering caves and generating some temporary income.

Gold tends to be the scarcest resource, while crystals can be useful for healing and mana potions. This situation occurs because you need to hire mercenary combat troops in the game's early stages, and gold is their favorite payment. You may be tempted to convert crystals into gold at your Capital, but the poor exchange rates at the Market tend to make trading them away a bad idea.

YOUR GOALS

Your goal in **Lords of Magic** is to defeat Balkoth. This may sound like a straightforward task, but there are a few important notes associated with this feat.

For one thing, you must realize that your goal is **not** to take over every other faith in the game. Assimilating other faiths helps you out in many ways, but you don't need to knock 'em all out before taking on Balkoth. In fact, Balkoth just may find **you** before you manage to deal with all the other faiths.

Also, it's important to realize that you don't need to siege the Death Capital or the Great Temple to win. If you kill Balkoth in the open field, victory is yours. Therefore, don't assume that you need to prepare for a big siege in Death territory—Balkoth often appears elsewhere.

Fig. 2-4. This army contains Balkoth. Kill Balkoth himself and you win—you don't even have to kill the rest of the army!

Finally, you need to understand that Balkoth's armies are, to some degree, irrelevant. An army without Balkoth is still a potential danger, but you should only attack if you are sure you can win. Destroying Balkoth's minions reduces Death's overall power somewhat and will give you valuable experience but Balkoth's personal army (figure 2-4) will not be affected—and that's the army you have to confront if you hope to win the game.

> **What about armies with Balkoth? If your army meets Balkoth's army and is crushed—but you manage to kill Balkoth himself in the battle—you'll win the game. (Of course, this assumes that your Lord managed to run away.) Even if your Lord is killed in the fray, you still win the game if you kill Balkoth and have one living heirs.**

EARLY MOVES

In a typical single-player game, your party starts out somewhere near your Capital. You have your Lord, a scouting unit, and a few assorted combat units in your party. These party members are loyal followers, therefore they are much cheaper than mercenaries.

Unfortunately, you need more muscle if you hope to succeed, and you don't have the resources or men necessary to train more loyal followers. You must, therefore, rely on mercenaries throughout the early stages of the game.

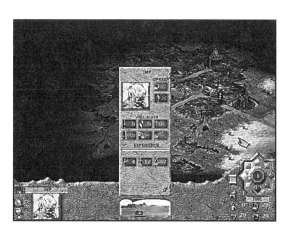

Fig. 2-5. This scouting unit needs to uncover the map, revealing low-level caves and mines for your main party to attack.

BREAK UP THE PARTY

The first order of business is to break up your party. Take your best scouting unit (usually a Thief or a true scout unit such as a Hound, Mite, or Imp) and have it wander off by itself (figure 2-5). Specifically, have the scouting unit start by exploring the terrain closest to your Capital. Have it start at the Capital itself and systematically spiral outward, running ever-larger circles around the Capital and exposing terrain that was once shrouded in blackness.

As your scout reveals new terrain, caves are bound to appear. Have your scout investigate these caves by walking into them. This lets you see the level of opposition in the cave (Level 1 or Level 4, for example). Of course, you don't actually want your scout to fight—that'd be suicide. All the scout needs to do is gauge the level of opposition in the cave.

Flying units are relatively common in Air. These units can freely cross large bodies of water and have additional mobility in combat. In general, Air units also tend to have great speed.

Air's spell repertoire is powerful and varied with many spells geared toward slowing down or immobilizing the enemy. It also has several potent attack spells capable of decimating enemy armies.

Air starts the game in a loose alliance with Life, Order, and Water.

> **BOTTOM LINE:** Air requires a player who wants a challenge and uses nonconventional tactics. It is a specialized faith but very good in its specialties, especially speed and maneuverability.

CHAOS

A brawler's faith, Chaos has infantry and cavalry that are capable of inflicting and receiving a great deal of punishment; however, their defensive skills are underdeveloped. Groups of Chaos soldiers can decimate an enemy before it has a chance to respond.

Chaos's missile troops are unusually durable, though their range is somewhat limited.

The Chaos spell book contains many spells with random effects. Frequently, these spells are very potent, but their random nature may hurt their caster more than help him. Many Chaos spells harm **both** sides of a battle.

Chaos starts the game in a loose alliance with Death, Earth, and Fire.

Generally speaking, you shouldn't go on to the next step (augmenting the party) until your scout has discovered at least one Level 1 cave—ideally two.

AUGMENT THE PARTY

Have your main party (the one with your Lord and assorted combat units) enter the local Barracks or Thieves' Guild. There they should purchase an extra combat unit to help with upcoming battles.

> Be sure not to hire a mercenary until your scout unit has uncovered a Level 1 cave. Your time will be extremely limited once you hire the mercenary unit; you must have a clear destination in mind before hiring.

Your Lord's class and faith should help you decide which mercenary type to hire. In general, cavalry is your best bet, as it combines good combat skills with great mobility—and in the early stages of the game, a slow army that takes extra turns to move from one place to another is a big waste of money. Each extra turn represents another payment to the mercenaries. The swifter your army, the better!

Infantry can also be a decent investment if your party already contains at least one slow unit. In this case, the infantry's lack of speed won't affect your already sluggish party. Missile attackers, such as Elven Archers and Fae Slingers, can also be a wise investment, especially if your faith has particularly strong missile troops or if your Lord is a Mage who can help the missile troops. A good example of this would be the Storm Lord, who can use his Headwind spell to slow enemies down and to give missile troops more time to shoot.

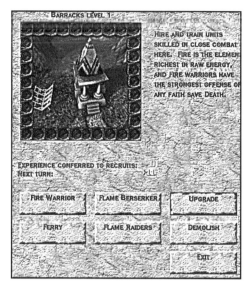

Fig. 2-6. Infantry (in this case, Flame Berserkers) and cavalry (in this case, Flame Raiders) are good choices for first mercenary units.

First-level Mages are almost never a good first addition to your party, as they don't have the mana or spells to help you out—at least, not at this stage of the game. Similarly, low-level Warrior and Thief Champions aren't numerous enough to help your war effort significantly. What you need at this point are several strong backs, and that usually translates into infantry or cavalry. (See figure 2-6.)

ASSAULT LOW-LEVEL CAVES

At this point your party has a little extra firepower, but has taken on some heavy financial responsibilities. Your mercenary troops are necessary, but they're also quite expensive. Their demands for gold and ale (particularly gold) make it imperative to generate some income over the next few turns. In a Medium-difficulty game, where you begin with 18 of each resource, you are likely to run out of gold three turns after hiring the mercenary. In a Hard game, you usually only have two turns to seek new income.

By this point, however, your scout has uncovered a nearby Level 1 cave. Send your main party in a beeline toward this structure. You may want to save the game before entering, though, because the success of your entire game currently hinges on this one tiny battle!

If you're lucky, you will win this initial battle without sustaining too many casualties. Equally important, however, is that you get a decent amount of loot. Treasure is somewhat random, so you may be surprised when a paltry group of enemies yields a fair amount of gold, or when a tough enemy band gives up a handful of coins. At the very least, you need to win enough gold to move along to the next cave. If you run out of resources along the way, your mercenaries will desert you.

If you consistently have a rough time with your first battle, refer to Chapter 4 for tips on successful combat. One particularly important tip from that chapter bears repeating here: **send your mercenaries to the forefront of battle whenever possible while keeping your loyal followers in relative safety.** That way the expensive mercenaries bear the brunt of enemy attacks, while your loyal troops (who cost less to maintain) stay—relatively—healthy.

Sometimes you'll win a battle, but the victory doesn't yield enough gold and ale to let you retain your mercenaries. In this case, you should reload from a previously saved game and either pick a different cave to attack (hopefully, one with a better resource payoff inside) or attack the same cave as before. The spoils from victories in caves are somewhat random. You may only get three ale the first time you attack a particular cave, but upon reloading a saved game and attacking again, the cave may yield six ale instead.

CONTINUE THE FIGHT; AUGMENT YOUR ARMY

What now? You need to keep attacking low-level caves in the vicinity of your Capital. Always go for the lowest-level caves you can find; higher-level caves are likely to decimate your troops without yielding enough gold and ale to replace them. By keeping your existing troops alive, you avoid the cost of constantly hiring new mercenaries. Your men also gain experience, and these experienced troops are much more valuable than fresh recruits.

Of course, you eventually need to hire new mercenaries as your army continues to ransack local caves. Existing troops will die and will need to be replaced. Some higher-level caves require more muscle to conquer, and at those points, you will need to add new mercenaries to your army.

When hiring new mercenaries, always follow these few simple guidelines:

1. Stick to infantry, cavalry, and missile troops—at least at first. Champions of all descriptions are useful once you have a solid foundation of regular troops, but you shouldn't expect them to be your army's core. They're superior to regular troops, but regular troops come in groups of three, giving your army the bulk it needs.

2. Don't hire mercenaries that will slow your party down. If you already have slow troops, feel free to add some more. But if your army is fast, you need to stick with fast troops to cut down on wasted turns.

3. Leave yourself enough gold and ale to pay your mercenaries for at least a couple of turns. There's nothing worse than hiring mercenaries and then finding yourself unable to pay them.

4. If your armies are injured in combat and you're employing mercenaries, either go to the temple or dismiss them. Don't let a mercenary sit in a cave to heal.

The early stages of the game require considerable mercenary micro-management. For example, if a mercenary unit is injured to the point where it's almost useless—an infantry group, for example, has only one sliver of health and one member left—you may have to dismiss it to cut costs. Sure, mercenaries eventually heal, but that doesn't mean you should pay them while they're useless!

CONQUER MINES IF POSSIBLE

As your army grows you should try to conquer nearby mines, like the one shown in figure 2-7. (Remember, we're using the word "mines" in the general sense, referring to any structure that produces resources: Crystal mines, Gold mines, or Breweries.)

Mines are fundamentally similar to caves, save that they generate a constant supply of resources every turn that they are under your control. One or two good mines can make the difference between early-game success and failure; you should always look for (and conquer) local mines as quickly as possible. If you see a cave and a mine that contain the same level of opposition, always try to conquer the mine first.

Fig. 2-7. This Brewery is considered a mine. Since it's a Level 6 mine, it produces six ale per turn for its owner.

CONQUER THE GREAT TEMPLE

By the time your army has swelled to include your Lord and at least four other combat units—preferably infantry or cavalry, and preferably healthy units at that—you may be ready to take on the Great Temple (figure 2-8). If your scout unit has searched the map diligently up to this point, he should have

Fig. 2-8. This monolithic statue is Order's Great Temple.

uncovered the Great Temple by now. The Great Temple is always within a couple days' walk of your Capital; thorough exploration in all directions always will locate it within the first ten turns.

Generally speaking, you should take over your Great Temple as soon as humanly possible. Some players like to save the game and then try to attack the Temple, reloading the game if they're unsuccessful and trying again later. Regardless of whether this technique appeals to you, it's indisputable that you need to take over that Temple as soon as you can. Before you take the Great Temple, you'll be living a hand-to-mouth existence. After you conquer it, you automatically receive ten loyal followers and the ability to gain more followers every week. Your conquest of the Great Temple is the single biggest event of the game's early stages; it catapults your game into high gear.

Great Temples generally aren't that tough to conquer—at least, your own isn't. Other faith's Great Temples tend to have more deadly bad guys lurking inside, but your own Temple has roughly the equivalent of a Level 2 force waiting for you. If your party can defeat a Level 2 cave, it probably can take over your Great Temple as well.

EMPIRE BUILDING

As soon as you have retaken your Great Temple, you're a full-fledged power in the land of Urak. You can now shift your attention partially away from caves and mines—although they're still an important part of the game—toward Urak's other faiths. You have entered the middle stages of the game, where your biggest task is to expand your sphere of influence and build your empire.

ALLOCATE FOLLOWERS

The instant you conquer the Great Temple your Capital receives a Level 1 Stronghold. You also receive ten followers to allocate as you wish. You

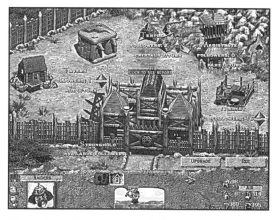

Fig. 2-9. Allocate loyal followers between several work places in your Stronghold.

should return to your Capital as quickly as possible to allocate these men (figure 2-9). Have them work in the Marketplace to earn gold, in the Temple to generate crystals, at the Magistrate's to generate fame, or in the Tavern to brew ale. Unused followers can be converted into loyal troops in the local Barracks, Thieves' Guild, or Mage Tower; however, it's recommended that you have most of your followers earn resources at this point in time. If you turn all of your followers into soldiers after all, your resource-building infrastructure will never grow! So, be sure that at least eight of your ten followers are put to work generating resources.

DESIGNATE SCOUTS

Just because you've conquered your Great Temple doesn't mean you should stop scouting the map. Indeed, you should have an additional unit start scouting to reveal more extensively the world around you. That way, when your armies are ready to march and help your empire expand, you will have uncovered suitable targets for them to attack.

If you received a Thief hero when you reclaimed your Great Temple, you can use this unit as an effective scout. If not, hiring a Thief Champion or a scouting unit from the local Thieves' Guild may be a good way to get an extra scout on the move.

DIVIDE YOUR TROOPS

Now that you've retaken your Great Temple and conquered many of the lowest-level caves and mines, you must decide what to do during the next few turns. Specifically, you need to figure out what to do with your main party. This force is largely composed of expensive mercenaries that prevent your faith from accumulating wealth—it's inadvisable to let them sit around.

Assuming that your scouts haven't found any big enemy forces roaming your lands, you could dismiss these mercenaries and remain dormant for several turns, simply accumulating wealth that otherwise would have gone to the mercenaries. But that's not a terribly efficient use of your time and gold. You have considerable gold and ale invested in your mercenaries, and to dismiss them is to waste those resources.

Instead of releasing your mercenary troops, use them to attack several more local caves and mines. If you manage to take over these locations with few losses, your mercenaries gain more experience, and they'll win enough gold to pay their own salaries. If they're decimated in the attack, you at least got some extra use out of them—and they'll no longer drain your resources. You'll then be able to build up wealth to replace mercenaries with loyal troops.

Your Lord should participate in most of these battles, resting and recovering in the structure appropriate to his class between forays. (In other words, a Warrior Lord should rest in the Barracks, while a Mage Lord recovers in the Mage Tower.) This allows the Lord to bestow experience points upon units recruited at the structure.

START RESEARCH IF NECESSARY

If you plan to engage in serious spell research, you need to hire a pair of Mage Champions as quickly as possible.

If your Lord is not a Mage, have your first Mage Champion start researching a useful spell in the Library. Meanwhile, have your second Mage Champion team up with your main army and gain a few levels. When this Champion has attained Level 2 or 3, he will be skillful enough to research low-level spells within a reasonable period of time. He can then take over the Library while the first Champion joins the main army.

Fig. 2-10. The Air Lord is busy researching spells, something he shouldn't do until the middle to late stages of the game.

By swapping places in this way, you can always have one Mage researching spells while the other gains experience.

If your Lord is a Mage, you should still hire two Mage Champions and have them divide research and combat tasks as explained above. Meanwhile, your Lord should participate in large battles, periodically spending time at the Mage Tower to confer his experience upon new recruits. When he's taught the Tower just about everything he can teach it, you can have him take over spell research or join your army for further conquests. (See figure 2-10.)

WHEN TO BUILD UP YOUR STRONGHOLD

After you have cleared out most of the nearby caves and have a good deal of resources stored up, the time is ripe for consolidation and training. A very important part of late-game strategy is being able to build units that do not start out at the first level. The first period of consolidation begins with the building of a level two stronghold and the upgrading of your other buildings if you have a fifth level (or higher) champion who can train units in that building.

At this point these units have gained enough experience that having them sit idle in a Barracks for 10 turns to impart 20 percent of their experience to the building is worth it. If you have a Mage training in such a manner, after the Mages' Tower has been maxed out for experience, begin your research with two Mages for greater research speed. The Mages' Tower is one of the most important buildings to upgrade because it allows you to build creatures that begin at higher levels than the troops you will be training. It also affects the number of Mages you can have researching.

PREPARE YOUR DEFENSES

Up until this point, you probably have had only a few Renegade parties to worry about. These Renegades consist of combat units from any given faith, but the Renegades are not truly affiliated with that faith. It doesn't matter whether you have good relations with their faith or not—Renegades will attack you just the same.

Renegades tend to attack completely undefended structures and avoid structures with anyone inside. Therefore, it's a good idea to have at least one unit camped at your Capital at all times.

It's not practical, however, to have a unit guarding every single structure in your possession (Capital, Barracks, Mage Tower, Thieves' Guild, mines, and so forth). The best you can hope for is to have someone in the general vicinity. Ideally, you should have a defensive army camped near each Capital under your control at all times. In practice, however, it's too expensive to maintain large armies in several places at the same time. You'll have to settle for very small armies, as shown in figure 2-11.

Fig. 2-11. This small army consists only of the Order Lord and a group of Crossbowmen. Since it can hire mercenaries from the Capital's outlying structures at any time, this small force is sufficient to keep the Capital secure.

LORDS OF MAGIC is a game that requires fast expansion and potent offense; you can't afford to have your biggest armies sitting around on defense. Nor can you afford to split up your armies into several small defensive patrols.

So what should you do? In many cases, you can get away with having a single fast unit on guard near each Capital under your control. When an enemy party starts to get dangerously close to one of your Capitals, this lone unit can visit any outlying buildings and purchase lots of mercenaries for a cheap, quick defense. You can disband the mercenaries once you no longer need them.

This technique requires you to have free resources to pay the mercenaries and works best if the local Barracks or Thieves' Guild has had experience bestowed upon it, allowing you to hire mercenaries at Level 2 or higher.

BE CAREFUL!

The whole point of attacking caves or mines after taking the Great Temple is to build up your army. Spend one or two weeks taking over caves and mines, and your army will gain more experience—plus you'll acquire more followers at your Stronghold. The end results are a tougher, more experienced army and the resources to train a few loyal followers.

Attacking caves, mines, and statues after liberating the Great Temple may, in fact, be COUNTERPRODUCTIVE, especially if your army is massacred in the process. Any battle that significantly weakens your army isn't helpful. Avoid these ultra-tough combats for now.

EXPAND YOUR EMPIRE

At some point, you have to expand your empire. Ideally, you should do this after accumulating at least a week's worth of new followers and assigning them to produce gold and other necessary resources. This allows your army to roam far and wide without running out of resources, forcing it to disband.

You should train other followers to be military units, increasing the size of your army to at least six units. This army may include a few fresh recruits, but it should have its fair share of veterans as well.

Your goal at this point is to take over another faith. This can be an easy matter or a difficult ordeal, depending on the game difficulty and on your relationship with the other faith.

The effects of a game's level of difficulty are obvious, but the role of attitude and of relationship is not. To take over a faith that you're on good terms with, all you need to do is conquer the other faith's Great Temple. To take over a hostile faith, you must conquer the faith's Great Temple and its Capital, and you must eliminate the enemy Lord in combat (not necessarily in that order). You also have to destroy all remaining units belonging to that faith, or they'll try to retake their Capital.

> Who should you attack first? If your army isn't that strong, attack the Great Temple of a friendly faith. Success automatically yields you another Capital and some free units, allowing you to jump-start your sluggish economy. If your army is fairly strong and a neighboring enemy faith is bugging you, try to take over its Great Temple and Capital, and try to defeat the enemy Lord in combat. If you succeed, you will have crushed an enemy AND gained a new Stronghold.

In either case, try to take over a bordering Village first. Taking over a Village and building a military structure there allow you to restock your army's troops without having to retreat all the way to your Capital. This also lets you fill in any holes, thereby accounting for your weaknesses.

ASSIMILATE ANOTHER FAITH

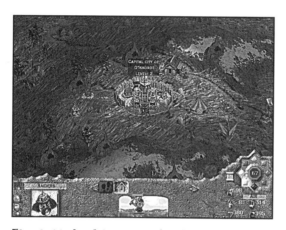

Fig. 2-12. In this game, Air has taken over its closest neighbors to the north and south, Order and Chaos. The Chaos Capital (pictured) is guarded by Chaos Raiders hired from the local Barracks.

You should try to absorb two neighboring faiths as quickly as possible, as the player in figure 2-12 has done. This assimilation gives you two extra Strongholds and considerable fame, allowing you to attract and allocate followers without constantly upgrading your initial Stronghold. These new Strongholds should be upgraded when necessary, but remember that the goal of your game isn't to build the best Strongholds. It's to beat the tar out of your opponents (especially Balkoth)! Only upgrade Strongholds and outlying structures when you see an **immediate, tangible benefit** for doing so. Note that expanding too quickly could leave your stronghold inadequetely protected.

LATE-GAME TECHNIQUES

As the later stages of the game wear on, the number of independent faiths gradually decreases. Just as you (hopefully) have assimilated one or more faiths by this time, so have other faiths. It is not uncommon to find out that, by turn 60 or 70, there are only four distinct sides to the battle for Urak—the other faiths have been destroyed or swallowed up by the faiths that still exist.

At this point in the game, you're free to pursue your own strategy. You have acquired enough resources to support a large army, and you have developed a sprawling empire that spans a good chunk of the world....

It's up to you whether to sit and wait for Balkoth or to meet him in his own lands.

CONTINUED EXPLORATION AND CONQUESTS

You should continue to attack mines, caves, and other structures scattered across the land. This keeps your main army in fighting form and allows it to grow continually in terms of experience. This also may provide fringe benefits, such as artifacts and extra resources. You may have several armies at this point, but you should try to maintain one army that stands above the rest. This main army should accompany your Lord wherever he goes and should keep him from being an easy target for enemy Lords. This is the army that, hopefully, will defeat Balkoth.

Meanwhile, your scouts should continue to roam across the map to uncover new terrain. This exploration allows you to keep tabs on what's going on in the world and—if you're lucky—to see where Balkoth is currently stationed. Good scouting lets you see attacks well before they arrive, giving you time to hire mercenaries, train new troops, or move existing armies into position to respond to the imminent threat.

> Turn on the Center on Movement option from the in-game Options menu. This allows you to see exactly what enemy units are doing. With this option turned off, it's easy to miss significant happenings, such as battles between two faiths or a big army headed straight for your Capital.

CONSOLIDATION

Taking over Great Temples and assimilating other faiths are useful for accumulating new followers that you can put to work. Rapid expansion, however, can't go on forever because some things simply can't be accomplished without spending some time at home. For example, you never will be able to hire your faith's highest-level summoned creatures without investing in your Stronghold and your Mage Tower; likewise, you never will learn any new spells without having Mages conduct research. Similarly, the units hired from your Barracks will never start at a higher level than Level 1 unless a Champion or Lord spends time there and imparts his wisdom upon the building. (See figure 2-13.)

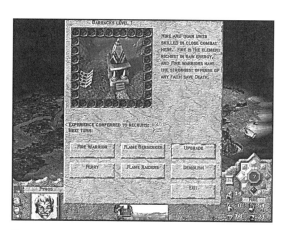

Fig. 2-13. The Lord of Fire imparts valuable knowledge upon a Barracks.

After you have taken over a modest chunk of the world—again, we recommend taking over two faiths—you should spend some time consolidating your gains. Upgrade Strongholds, Barracks, Thieves' Guilds, and Mage Towers. Have your Lords or Champions bestow experience upon key structures. And send your Mages to research spells in the Library. In this way, you will be able to muster the high-level spells, troops, and summoned creatures necessary for your final confrontation with Balkoth.

DEALING WITH BALKOTH

After you have researched a few great spells or summoned some high-level creatures, you'll be itching for a fight. Your have four choices: (1) seek out Balkoth, (2) wait for him to attack you, (3) take over other faiths in the meantime, or (4) in your own territory, attack mid- or high-level caves to gain arti-facts, money, and experience. All three methods are discussed in this section.

> If you want specific tips on the tactics of beating Balkoth, refer to Chapter 6, which explains the basics of when and where to initiate the fight.

ATTACKING BALKOTH

Your toughest option is to take Balkoth on on his own turf. (See figure 2-14.) It's tough because you probably will encounter a few of Balkoth's smaller armies before meeting the evil Lord himself. These armies may just soften up your army to the point where it's not strong enough to beat him.

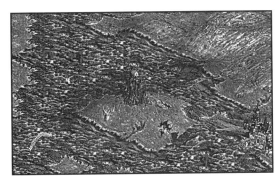

Fig. 2-14. Balkoth's home territory of charred rock and black ash is a formidable place to visit. Don't go there unless you're extremely confident in your army's superiority.

Also, attacking Balkoth in his own territory allows him to buy reinforcements or to retreat into his Stronghold for better defense. On the other hand, you'll be far away from your own reinforcements.

The only reasons to attack Balkoth in his own territory are as follows:

1. Your army is so tough that you know you're ready to fight Balkoth.

2. You think Balkoth's army may not be in great shape, and you want to press the advantage.

3. You're too impatient for your own good.

In most situations, you should let Balkoth come to you instead of carrying the fight to him.

WAITING FOR BALKOTH

Balkoth roams the map just like any other Lord. It's a pretty sure bet that he'll show up on your doorstep with a big nightmarish army in tow at **some** point. The primary downside to Balkoth's sudden appearance is that it's difficult to predict. The advantage is that you will be in a better position to deal with him than you would be in his homeland.

When Balkoth enters your turf, you can summon or hire a bunch of auxiliary forces just to soften him up. Furthermore, your existing troops are likely to be somewhere nearby. You can have your Lord flee until the reserves appear and **then** attack. Your Lord can also retreat inside your Level 3 Stronghold to use the gates for extra protection.

TAKING OVER MORE FAITHS

The third option is to avoid Balkoth for the time being and concentrate on taking over other faiths. What's the benefit to this? Well, if you only take over two faiths and then wait indefinitely for Balkoth, he may take over all the remaining faiths while you just twiddle your thumbs. According to simple arithmetic, the end result would be that Balkoth has five faiths under his control, while you have only three. This would allow Balkoth to generate resources faster than you, and consequently, he also would build armies faster than you. You can't let that happen!

If you have been waiting for Balkoth—and he doesn't show up—you should consider taking over another faith. That way, you'll have at least four faiths—at the very least, you'll be even with Balkoth.

Another option is to build your strength by attacking caves, dungeons, and towers. These places are great sources of experience for your armies, as well as a source of artifacts and more treasure. Artifacts can give your armies an important edge in a close fight.

ONWARD TO BATTLE!

If it seems as if we haven't given you the whole scoop in this chapter, you're exactly right! This chapter was just a rough outline of how to approach your goals. It's enough to give you a head start in your first few games of **Lords of Magic.** Keep on reading, and you'll learn more specific information on how the game works and how to beat it.

CHAPTER

THE INNER WORKINGS OF URAK

s you're playing **Lords of Magic**, you may find yourself wondering exactly how things work. How do you accumulate followers? How does terrain affect the game? How do various structures differ from one another? This chapter explains some of the most fundamental features of **Lords of Magic** and gives you a better sense of what's going on behind the scenes every time you play a game.

TERRAIN

Every faith in **Lords of Magic** has its own terrain type. Units belonging to a given faith can travel marginally faster on their native terrain type than on other faiths' terrain (usually just one or two points per turn). If you have doubts about what your faith's terrain looks like, simply examine the ground around your faith's Capital and Great Temple.

Hills and steep inclines tend to devour movement points quickly. This can lead to confusion and miscalculation when you first start playing. For example, you may think your party is only one turn's walk from an object or an enemy, but in reality, a steep incline makes it a two- or three-turn trip.

After playing for a while, you learn how to judge distances accurately. You also learn to plan your units' travels in such a way that they avoid hills and mountains, unless it's absolutely necessary to travel there.

> It's often best to click right on the place you want your units to go instead of setting smaller, intermediate way points for them. You'll discover that the use of way points is seldom productive, as clicking on the final destination point usually results in the unit taking the best possible path.

FURTHER EFFECTS OF TERRAIN

Ships, Water units, and Air's flying units can traverse lakes and oceans, while other units are stuck on land. The exception to this rule is rivers, which can sometimes be forded at narrow points by any unit type. Fording rivers tends to eat up movement points quickly, so prepare for a long wait as your units struggle across.

> Parties that are out of movement points can't cast spells even if they possess the mana to do so. Similarly, parties out of movement points can't interact with structures—even if they're inside a structure.

Roads are found throughout Urak, connecting Capitals to their outlying structures and occasionally spanning large sections of terrain (figure 3-1). Your units receive a hefty movement bonus when they travel on roads. This accounts for the unusual pheno-menon where your units seem capable of traveling vast distances when close to home, yet are mysteri-ously slow when venturing out into the wilderness.

Fig. 3-1. Use roads whenever possible. You'll always find roads connecting Capitals to outlying structures.

Make use of roads whenever possible, and try to account for their effects when you plan troop move-ments. This is especially important in the early game when every move is crucial. By using roads, you often will find that your units can reach a seemingly distant cave faster than one that appears to be closer. Click on different destinations, and the game automatically calculates travel time. Gauge how many turns are necessary to reach any given destination, and pick your best travel option accordingly.

COMBAT TERRAIN

When you engage in combat, it takes place on a battle map representative of the section of the world map that the fight was initiated on. For example, if you start a fight on the plains, your battle map will be relatively flat. If you initiate a battle in the mountains, rocky terrain appears on the battle map. And if you begin a battle at sea, the battle is fought on water.

Combat in a stronghold usually favors the defender, as higher-level strongholds have better solid defensive fortifications. Also, note that battles between land-based and water-based units take place on a battle map half-covered with water. If the land-based units can't fly and can't hurl spells or missiles, it's entirely possible that they can't do anything to damage their seafaring opponents.

IMPORTANT STRUCTURES

Urak's landscape is dotted with important structures. Here's a look at what you can expect to find as your parties traverse the land.

CAPITALS

When each faith starts the game, it possesses a single Capital. Before a faith's Great Temple is liberated, the Capital doesn't have a Stronghold. After you liberate the Temple, a Level 1 Stronghold appears inside the Capital.

Strongholds have sturdy walls useful for defense. More importantly, they allow you to gather followers and allocate them to various tasks, such as gold, ale, and crystal production. Finally, Strongholds contain intelligence reports on other faiths.

Taking over another faith's Capital lets you access the outlying structures (Barracks, Library, etc.) of that Capital. It does not, however, give you an automatic victory over the faith whose Capital you have captured. To assimilate a friendly faith, you must take over its Great Temple. If a faith happens to be hostile toward your own faith, you need to take over the faith's Capital and Great Temple and crush its Lord in combat.

While taking an enemy Capital does not give you control of a particular faith, it does have certain major repercussions. Taking over an enemy faith's Capital allows you to assume control of the followers assigned to work in that Capital and prevents the enemy from recruiting new troops at local outlying structures.

A key to winning the game is to take over several faiths' Capitals, giving you a number of different places to allocate followers.

OUTLYING STRUCTURES

Each Capital is surrounded by several outlying structures: A Barracks, a Thieves' Guild, a Mages' Tower, and a Library. These structures can be used by the faith currently in control of the Capital.

If a Renegade party—or, in fact, any enemy party—enters one of these outlying structures and occupies it for more than one turn, that structure can be completely destroyed. This means that the owner must pay to rebuild the structure back to Level 1 if he hopes to use it in the future. If the structure was previously at Level 2 or Level 3, its destruction can be a devastating blow.

BARRACKS

Barracks are the primary source of melee (hand-to-hand) combatants. In the Barracks, you may hire the following unit types:

Warrior Champion (e.g., Fire Warrior)

Infantry (e.g., Flame Berserkers)

Cavalry (e.g., Flame Raiders)

Ship (e.g., Ferry)

You may hire these unit types from a Barracks of any level. Higher-level Barracks are capable of producing higher-level units. (See the Experience section later in this chapter for more details.)

THIEVES' GUILD

The Thieves' Guild produces Thief-type units. Specifically, you can hire the following unit types:

Thief Champion (e.g., Dwarven Thief)

Missile Troops (e.g., Rockhurlers)

Scouting Unit (e.g., Imp)

As with the Barracks, all unit types are available regardless of the structure's level. Higher-level Thieves' Guilds simply bestow more experience upon new recruits.

MAGES' TOWER

A Mages' Tower is the place to hire Mages and magical creatures. Here's what you can hope to find at the local Mages' Tower:

Mage Champion (e.g., Fire Sorceress)

Potions (Items that allow Mages to recover mana)

Level 1 Summoned Creatures (e.g., Fire Elemental)

Level 2 Summoned Creatures (e.g., Demon)

There are a few major differences between the Mages' Tower and other outlying structures. For one thing, some units are unavailable for hire at lower-level Mages' Towers. Specifically, a Level 1 Mages' Tower offers Mage Champions but no other units. When the Mages' Tower is upgraded to Level 2, it contains Level 1 summoned creatures; a Level 3 Mages' Tower has Level 2 summoned creatures, as shown in figure 3-2. (Level 3 summoned creatures appear at the Great Temple after you upgrade the Mages' Tower to Level 3.)

When you upgrade a Mages' Tower, you increase the potential experience bestowed upon new Mage Champions recruited there. Summoned creatures, however, do not benefit from this experience bonus because

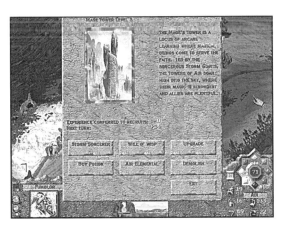

Fig. 3-2. This Air Mages' Tower has been upgraded to Level 3; hence, you can summon both Will O' Wisps and Air Elementals here.

summoned creatures **never** gain experience or levels.

Upgrades to Mages' Towers have a direct effect on Libraries. See the next section for details.

LIBRARIES

Libraries are the only places where spell research takes place. Libraries themselves cannot be upgraded, but they do change to reflect upgrades in their associated Mages' Tower. Upgrading the local Mages' Tower to Level 2 adds a second research desk to the Library, and upgrading to Level 3 adds a third research desk. A Library associated with a Level 3 Mages' Tower can have three Mages researching inside at the same time, as opposed to the usual limit of one.

GREAT TEMPLES

In many ways, Great Temples are the key to **Lords of Magic.** By taking control of your own faith's Great Temple, you automatically build a Stronghold, gain ten followers, and turn your faith into a legitimate power. By taking control of a friendly faith's Great Temple, you assume control of that faith.

Great Temples are responsible for attracting new followers to a particular faith. If the enemy takes control of your Great Temple, you won't receive the usual weekly influx of followers until you retake it. Similarly, taking over an enemy faith's Great Temple effectively cuts off its inflow of new followers.

Level 3 summoned creatures are purchased at the Great Temple. You must upgrade your Mages' Tower to Level 3 before these summoned creatures are available for hire at the Great Temple.

Conquering friendly faith's Great Temples is the easiest way to expand your empire. Conquering enemies, however, is usually better than overtaking a Great Temple—even though it's more difficult—because the end result is one less enemy for you to deal with.

VILLAGES

Villages (figure 3-3) appear at the border between two faiths. If you manage to take over a Village, you can build a single military structure (Barracks, Thieves' Guild, or Mages' Tower) there. This structure can be of either faith that the Village borders. For example, you could build an Air or Order Barracks in a Village between Air and Order territories.

To build a military structure, you need to have a Champion or Lord that corresponds to that type of structure. In other words, a Warrior would build a Barracks at a Village, while a Thief would build a Thieves' Guild.

Fig. 3-3. This Village borders Air and Order. An Order Barracks has been built here for restocking purposes.

Here are some important tips on Villages:

- Villages can only support a single military structure at one time.

- To build military structures in a Village, you must be in control of one of the two faiths the Village borders.

- You can raze Villages if you think your enemies will use them against you, preventing further military structures at that Village.

- Any military structure you build in a Village can't be upgraded past the level of your nearest Capital's stronghold. If your nearest Capital's stronghold is Level 2, for example, that level (Level 2 in this case) serves as the limit for how high you can upgrade your military structure.

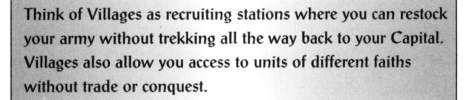

Think of Villages as recruiting stations where you can restock your army without trekking all the way back to your Capital. Villages also allow you access to units of different faiths without trade or conquest.

CAVES

Caves are enemy hideouts, pure and simple. Conquering a cave doesn't give you any special rewards. After combat takes place in caves, your only reward is the usual spoils from slain enemies and the experience points you earn.

Caves are ranked with levels of difficulty. A Level 1 cave is easily beaten, while a Level 8 cave is nearly impossible for all but the most veteran parties. Combat difficulty in caves increases greatly from one level to the next. Don't be surprised if a party that can easily handle Level 3 caves has great difficulty tackling Level 4 caves.

Caves also serve as hiding spots. When your army is sitting in a cave, enemies can't see what sort of troops you have hidden inside. Conversely, when roaming enemies enter caves, you can't see the exact composition of their forces. This detail takes on additional significance in multiplayer games, where caves can be used to stage effective ambushes.

> You'll spend much of the game's early stages cleaning out caves. They aren't anything special, but they're a good source of income and a good place to hang out while you heal.

MINES

When we discuss mines, we actually refer to three different types of structures: Gold mines, Crystal mines, and Breweries. These structures are much like caves but with one major exception: mines provide its owner with a resource bonus every turn. As you may expect, Gold mines provide gold; Crystal mines provide crystals; and Breweries provide ale.

The exact amount of resources generated by a mine each turn depends on its level. A Level 3 Gold mine generates three gold (units) per turn, while a Level 2 Brewery produces two ale (units) per turn.

If you lose control of a mine to another faith, that faith gains the benefits of the mine.

> Take over mines whenever possible. They're especially vital in the game's early stages when you have to fight for every possible resource. Later in the game, your loyal followers will produce resources, but it's still nice to have the extra boost of several (conquered) mines.

STATUES

Statues are like mines, except that, instead of generating resources every turn, they generate fame.

TOWERS

Just like caves, towers are enemy strongholds. Towers tend to have tougher opponents than the average cave.

The main thing that sets towers apart from caves, however, is that they always yield a scroll, prisoner, or artifact when you beat the monsters hiding inside them. This is in addition to the regular spoils you get from defeating the creature.

DUNGEONS

Dungeons, like towers and caves, are lairs with tough enemies. Dungeons tend to have the toughest enemies of all the structure types; however, there's a big payoff if you manage to defeat a dungeon's inhabitants. After defeating the dungeon's denizens, you receive a major artifact as well as the usual spoils of war.

> Generally speaking, you should avoid dungeons until your empire has grown quite large with an incredibly tough main army. Have your army attack dungeons to build up experience points quickly and to gather artifacts that will be useful for your final confrontation with Balkoth.

UPGRADES

Upgrading structures is an important part of every game, but you shouldn't upgrade structures indiscriminately. Instead, stick to upgrading the structures that will yield tangible benefits. Although we have already covered some of this ground, here's a quick list of benefits realized from upgrading different structures:

Stronghold: Each Stronghold upgrade doubles the number of followers that can be assigned to a given area, such as the Marketplace or Magistrate. A Level 1 Stronghold can have eight followers in each area, a Level 2 Stronghold 16 followers, and a Level 3 Stronghold 32 followers.

Level 2 Strongholds gain a defensive wall, while Level 3 Strongholds acquire a gate that further adds to defense.

Your outlying structures cannot be upgraded above the level of your Stronghold; upgrading the Stronghold gives you more flexibility and options.

Outlying Structures: Higher level structures can contain more experience. (See the Experience section later in this chapter.)

Upgrading the Mages' Tower gives access to powerful summoned creatures.

Table 3-1 shows the expense of upgrading various structures. Note that outlying structures always begin at Level 1. Renegades or enemy faiths can raze these structures. When this happens, they must be rebuilt to Level 1 before they're useful again.

TABLE 3-1. UPGRADE EXPENSES

	Stronghold	Barracks	Mages' Tower	Thieves' Guild
Level 1	—	25 Gold, 25 Crystals	25 Crystals, 15 Ale, 10 Gold	35 Gold, 15 Crystals
Level 2	150 Gold, 50 Ale, 50 Crystals, 5 Followers	65 Ale, 55 Gold, 1 Follower	75 Crystals, 40 Ale, 15 Gold, 1 Follower	90 Gold, 40 Crystals, 1 Follower
Level 3	500 Gold, 225 Ale, 225 Crystals, 12 Followers	175 Ale, 85 Gold, 3 Followers	150 Crystals, 60 Ale, 25 Gold, 3 Followers	175 Gold, 60 Crystals, 3 Followers

UNIT TYPES

Each faith has 14 distinct unit types, which are marginally different from the other faiths' units. Some are better attackers while others are better defenders; some are fast while others are slow. Chapter 7 gives the hard details on every unit in the game, but for now, we will give you a brief overview of the 14 different unit types and their **typical** characteristics.

LORDS

Warrior Lord

Mage Lord

Thief Lord

Each faith starts with one Lord. These units are irreplaceable—they cannot be hired or trained.

Lords are similar to Champions, save that they can attain Level 12 (instead of topping out at Level 10). Generally superior to Champions and conventional combat units, Lords can use artifacts. They also gain levels faster than conventional combat units do.

CHAMPIONS

Warrior Champion

Mage Champion

Thief Champion

Champions are essentially toned-down Lords that can reach a maximum level of ten. Like Lords, they too can use artifacts and attain a very high level of combat ability. Unlike the case with Lords, though, you can hire or train an unlimited number of Champions.

CONVENTIONAL UNITS

Infantry

Cavalry

Missile Troops

Each faith has its own infantry and cavalry (both available from the Barracks) and missile troops (available from the Thieves' Guild); these units usually come in groups of three. While Champions and Lords are individually superior to conventional units, the conventional units' superior numbers are hard to argue with.

Infantry and cavalry tend to be good in melee combat. Cavalry is often less durable than infantry, but its superior speed and offensive capabilities allow you to build fast armies. Speed is especially key during the game's early stages.

Missile troops are typically quite fragile. They need to kill their enemies from a distance, or they risk being cut down instantly in melee combat. Still, large groups of missile troops rank among the game's most formidable opponents. They can cut down enemies before they get close and can avoid sustaining damage in return.

SUMMONED CREATURES

Summoned Creature 1

Summoned Creature 2

Summoned Creature 3

The two lower-level creatures are summoned at the Mages' Tower, while the highest-level creature is summoned at the Great Temple. Upgrades to the Mages' Tower are necessary before these units can be summoned.

Summoned creatures cannot advance in level. For purposes of game calculations, the two lower-level summoned creatures are treated as if they were third and fifth levels, respectively. The third summoned creature—the one summoned at the Great Temple—is treated as if it were at the eighth level.

> **There are exceptions to this rule. For example, the three fire creatures are treated as if they are at the fifth, eighth, and tenth levels.**

Summoned creatures are quite skilled in combat, and even the weakest one fares well against low-level conventional troops. Summoned creatures tend to have a resistance to the magic of certain faiths and, thus, can be incredibly effective at fighting units of those faiths.

MISCELLANEOUS UNITS

Scout Unit

Ship

Each faith has its own scout unit (hired at the Thieves' Guild) and ship (hired at the Barracks). Neither unit is capable of advancing in level, and both are considered to be Level 1 units.

The Scout unit is small and virtually useless in combat, but its excellent speed makes it good for overland exploration. Scouts can also be used in other roles—for example, to guard a Capital while the army is gone and to hire mercenaries for a quick defense should the need arise.

Ships are very fast. Their abilities to cross seas and to see a great distance make them good scouts as well as an excellent transport for armies.

EXPERIENCE

Most units can advance in level. To do so, they must gain a certain number of experience points either through combat or by special means described in the following pages. Note that Thieves do not gain experience for stealing, and Mages do not gain experience for casting spells. Combat is the only reliable way of racking up experience points.

COMBAT EXPERIENCE

At the beginning of combat, **Lords of Magic** assesses each side of the battle. It automatically generates a "pool" of experience based on the number and level of each side's units. When one side wins, it gains the other side's experience pool.

Experience from the enemy pool is divided among the victorious party's members. A huge army tends to gain experience slowly because there are many units to divide the experience between. On the other hand, a small army gains levels quickly because experience isn't spread as thinly as it is with larger armies. You will see this principle in action if you happen to fight an epic battle in which only one of your units manages to survive. The lucky surviving unit receives all the experience from the entire enemy pool and, consequently, is very likely to gain a level (perhaps, even two).

STRUCTURE EXPERIENCE

When a Champion or Lord spends time in his corresponding building (Barracks for Warriors, Mages' Tower for Mages, and Thieves' Guild for Thieves), that Champion or Lord bestows some of his experience upon the building. Any Champion or Lord bestowing experience in this way is called a Steward.

While the Steward remains in the structure, experience gradually accumulates; this experience is automatically bestowed upon new recruits trained or hired at that structure. This experience does not diminish over time and remains the same even as new units are hired. Therefore, once a Steward has imparted a certain number of experience points upon a structure, all new recruits from that point onward are guaranteed to receive this bonus.

A first-level structure can hold 10 percent of a Steward's total experience; a second-level structure 20 percent; and, a third-level 30 percent. Regardless of the structure's level or the Steward's experience, the Steward can always bestow his maximum experience benefit in 10 turns.

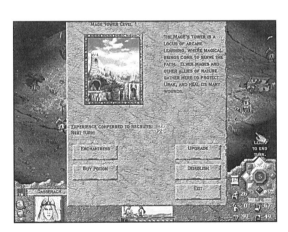

Fig. 3-4. This Mages' Tower contains 40 experience. 40 experience will be added to it on the next turn if the Air Lord stays there.

The current amount of experience stored in a structure is plainly listed inside the structure itself (figure 3-4). Also listed is the amount of experience (if any) that the Steward will bestow on the structure if he stays another turn.

FAME

Your faith receives an influx of new initiates every seven days, assuming that you have a Stronghold, of course. Before you have a Stronghold, you won't receive any initiates at all.

The Great Temple is what attracts most of your initiates. Therefore, if your faith possesses a Stronghold, but your Great Temple has been lost—to Renegades or an enemy faith, for example—you will only receive a fractional influx of weekly followers.

How many initiates will you receive in any given week? There are three main components to this equation.

1. You receive a fixed number of weekly followers based on the following scale:

Fame	35	70	140	280	560	950	2,100	4,200	8,400
Initiates	1	2	3	4	5	6	7	8	9

If you have 565 fame, for example, you receive four initiates. If you have 4,300 fame, you get seven initiates.

2. You also receive a number of followers equal to your total Stronghold level. If you have a single Level 1 Stronghold, you get one follower. If you have one Level 3 Stronghold, you receive three followers; and, if you own a Level 3 Stronghold and a Level 2 Stronghold, you receive a total of five followers (three for the first Stronghold and two for the second).

3. Finally, you get bonus followers based on what you did this week. Specifically, you receive an additional initiate for every 20 points of fame earned in the last seven days. If, for example, you happen to earn 82 fame in one week, you get four additional followers (82 divided by 20 is approximately 4) at the week's end.

INTELLIGENCE AND BARTER

Much of the time you'll be fighting with the other faiths of Urak, but you can't fight everyone—at least, not all at once. You must keep your relations with several faiths friendly, if only to keep them all from pouncing on you.

The following sections explain intelligence and barter, two primary tools in understanding and affecting relations with other faiths.

THE INTELLIGENCE REPORT

The Intelligence Report (figure 3-5), which is available at your Stronghold, provides information on the other faiths' military strength, resources, artifacts, and spell knowledge. This information ranges from reliable to completely inaccurate, and it's based largely on your previous dealings with each faith. These dealings include barter, combat, spying, and prisoner torture/interrogation. Information on your allies tends to be more accurate than information on your enemies, as you automatically receive bonus information when you're on good terms with a particular faith.

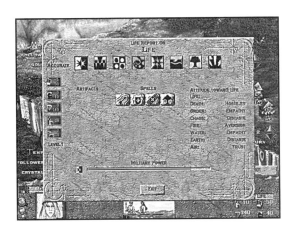

Fig. 3-5. Here's the Intelligence Report available at your Stronghold.

The more recent your interactions with a given faith, the more accurate your information will be. As time wears on, previously reliable information tends to lose its accuracy. A phrase on the upper left side of the Intelligence Report describes the accuracy of your information—you don't have to worry about being misled.

RESOURCES REPORT

The column running down the left side of the Intelligence Report provides information on the selected faith's resources. The bottom number within a particular resource is an estimate of the selected faith's total holdings, and the top number shows the change to these holdings per turn (based on the faith's estimated income and expenses). The level of this faith's Stronghold is shown below the resource information.

ARTIFACTS AND SPELLS

In the center of the report, there are headings for artifacts and spells. As your intelligence on a particular faith increases, symbols may appear under these headings, which represent the acquired artifacts and spell knowledge of a particular faith. If you engage in combat with another faith—and that faith uses spells or artifacts against you—this information will be transferred to your Intelligence Report.

ATTITUDES

On the right side of the Intelligence Report is a column that describes each faith's attitude toward the selected faith. Other faiths' attitudes toward you will change depending on their base affinity toward you modified by any barter, combat, and spying that occurs between you and that particular faith.

Political attitudes between faiths are divided into eleven stages, ranging from good to bad as follows:

Devotion Pact Kinship Trust Empathy Neutral Distaste Aversion Hostility Hatred Loathing

Table 3-2 explains how different faiths feel about one another at the beginning of a typical game. Relations between faiths are expressed numerically from 1 to 6. A 1 means that relations between the two faiths verge on hatred, while a 6 indicates that the faiths are on very good terms.

TABLE 3-2. INITIAL FAITH ATTITUDES

	Water	Fire	Earth	Air	Life	Death	Chaos	Order
Water	—	1	2	4	5	3	4	4
Fire	1	—	4	2	2	5	6	2
Earth	2	4	—	1	3	6	4	4
Air	4	2	1	—	6	2	2	6
Life	5	2	3	6	—	1	3	5
Death	3	5	6	2	1	—	5	3
Chaos	4	6	4	2	3	5	—	1
Order	4	2	4	6	4	2	1	—

MILITARY POWER

The bottom of the Intelligence Report is an estimate of the selected faith's military power (indicated by a temperature bar). The two vertical black brackets within the temperature bar represent your information's range of accuracy.

BARTER

Bartering is the only significant form of political expression in Urak. There are no pacts or alliances, no agreements or accords. There's only the ability to make deals that favor one side or another or deals that profit both sides equally. These deals always have political ramifications. But how, specifically, can you improve relations with a barter?

If a representative of another faith approaches you and offers a deal, feel free to give him something extra—something beyond the original terms of the deal. This helps win the other side's favor.

On the other hand, if you initiate the trade, you may want to set the tone to Gift instead of Trade. A Gift produces more political good will than a favorable Trade.

Each faith has a different idea of what constitutes a good trade. Generally speaking, if you want to stay in good favor with another faith you should be up front about your deals. If you offer a gift, call it a Gift; if it's a Trade, call it a Trade. If it's really a Request, then call it such. Don't pretend that a one-sided deal is a Trade because Trades are supposed to be fair.

> Trades and Gifts are good ways to improve relations with other faiths. Requests are also acceptable, although constantly requesting favors is seldom a good idea.
>
> Demands and Threats, conversely, are only suitable if you don't care what the other faith thinks of you. Pleas also tend to erode relationships, as they make your faith seem helpless and dependent.

THIEF ACTIVITIES

Thief activities are described in detail in the game manual. Here are a few additions and tips on these activities:

- When you detect another player's Thief trying to be stealthy, a crosshair graphic appears on the Thief (figure 3-6). This Thief isn't necessarily trying to do you harm...but he may be.

Fig. 3-6. This hiding Thief has been detected in combat; hence, the crosshair.

- When one of your Thieves is detected, the same crosshair graphic appears on him. This lets you know that your Thief isn't succeeding at his attempted stealth.

- Level differences are the most important factor in any thieving activity. Try to be sure that you have a level advantage over any units your Thief steals from, sneaks up on, or gathers intelligence from.

- The best way to detect enemy Thieves is with high-level Thieves of your own.

- Thieves can hide in combat **and** on the world map.

- Skillful Thieves can hide before fleeing from battle, often allowing them to escape without sustaining any damage whatsoever.

- Capitals have their own innate detection abilities. Think twice before sending a low-level Thief near a Capital.

MAGIC AND COMBAT

Specific tips on the inner workings of magic and combat appear in later chapters (chapters 4 and 5, respectively).

CHAPTER

4

COMBAT

ombat in **Lords of Magic** is relatively simple to understand, but that doesn't mean you'll master it instantly. This chapter illustrates the subtleties and peculiarities of combat in **Lords of Magic** and will help you become a better general.

WHEN TO FIGHT

Your first big decision is whether to start a fight at all. Sometimes you have no choice, but often, the decision is entirely in your hands. The following sections offer suggestions on when and when not to initiate combat.

FIGHT FOR RESOURCES

First and foremost, you should fight for resources. During the game's earliest stages, you need to fight for gold, ale, and crystals—the game's most basic resources. In later stages, you must fight to liberate your Great Temple and to conquer other Faiths. This gives you access to even greater resources; namely, new territory, Strongholds, and followers.

Secondary resources are fame, experience, and artifacts. It's perfectly legitimate to fight a battle solely for these things as all three will help you build better armies and succeed in the long run. Ideally, you should try to fight in battles that only offer a good combination of potential rewards. For example, instead of simply attacking a cave that may yield gold, ale, crystals, fame, experience, and artifacts, attack a mine that will yield a constant flow of resources, too.

FIGHT WINNABLE BATTLES

Try to fight "pushover" battles that don't offer much resistance. These battles provide incremental experience points and resource gains for minimal risk; hence, it is better to spend your army's time fighting these easy battles than to let them lie completely idle. The only time you **shouldn't** fight such battles is when you have something better to do instead or when you have to go out of your way to fight them. In these cases, you're better off avoiding the fight.

AVOID TOUGH CONFLICTS AND SMALL PRIZES

In general, engaging in battles that may cause serious harm to your army is a bad idea. Ideally, you want to start out fighting Level 1 opposition and **then** proceed **gradually** to Level 2, Level 3, and so forth. Attacking a Level 5 mine before your army is large and experienced is a great way to lose units and impair your war effort.

If there is anything worse than attacking a Level 5 mine, it's attacking a Level 5 cave like the one in figure 4-1! You have less to win—and just as much to lose—if you attack a cave at that level. Remember: Always fight for big resources, such as Strongholds and Great Temples, above all else; pick and choose winnable battles after that.

Fig. 4-1. One of the biggest decisions you must make is not how to fight but WHEN to fight. Attacking this Level 5 cave with a weak party is DEFINITELY NOT a good idea.

BUILDING ARMIES

Individual units have unique strengths and weaknesses, which are covered in detail in chapters 6 and 7. Individual unit abilities aside, there are a few simple rules you can follow to build and maintain a quality army. Follow these rules until you have played enough to have a good sense of how combat works. At that point, you'll have a good idea of when you can bend the rules and still be successful.

MELEE TROOPS FIRST

Champions are fun. Superior to standard troops in terms of raw combat ability, they can use artifacts, and they possess skills that the average combat unit doesn't have. Despite all these remarkable assets, you shouldn't put too many of them in your armies. Infantry and cavalry have one big plus that Champions can't duplicate—numbers.

Typical battles are decided by large contingents of melee troops clashing with each other, while support units hang back and assist melee troops in any way they can. You need infantry and cavalry to form the basis of your melee armies—Warrior Champions alone won't cut it. You can't put enough Champions in a single party to make an effective fighting force, and even if you could, they would be much more expensive than a comparable number of standard units. What you need is a large number of infantry and cavalry.

Highly unusual armies without these troop types are possible of course, but they require a special mix of units. For example, a large army composed entirely of missile troops supported by Mages can, under some circumstances, be deadly. In general, however, your armies need melee troops (infantry and cavalry) if they're to have any staying power. Without infantry and cavalry, the enemy can walk right up to your Mages and missile troops and cut them down at close range.

SUPPORT TROOPS SECOND

Mages and missile troops are often referred to as support troops because their job is to support infantry and cavalry. These units usually aren't tough enough to outlast an enemy army by themselves, but their spells and missiles help weaken the enemy to the point where your melee troops can finish them off easily.

As stated previously, armies comprised entirely of support troops sometimes work, but they typically fall apart when they face a strong contingent of melee troops.

Alternately, cavalry and infantry can be used to support Mages and missile units while they deal damage to units from afar. This is useful when playing Life, Order, or Death.

MAINTAIN A "KILLER ARMY"

Once you have assembled a potent army, keep it together. As the game progresses, you may find yourself in possession of numerous small armies, but it's important to have at least one super-powerful army stacked to the limit with potent veteran troops. Don't break up this army! Sometimes it may be tempting to dismantle armies and send parts of them to different spots for defensive purposes, but this usually just weakens your forces to the point where they are no longer useful. A single massive army may travel slowly, and it certainly can't be everywhere at once. But it's likely to be victorious when it **does** get into position—and that's what matters most.

PRESERVE VETERANS

You should make every effort to preserve your veteran units. These high-level units cannot be bought or trained; hence, they are quite difficult to replace. You should do your best to keep them alive in combat. Have them retreat behind the main combat line whenever they are badly injured, and have mercenaries take the brunt of enemy attacks whenever possible (instead of risking your loyal veterans).

Even if two members of a three-member infantry, cavalry, or missile unit are killed, the unit eventually "regrows" its lost members if it heals to its maximum health capacity. Therefore, you should **always** have a three-member unit that has lost two of its members retreat (unless the battle is going badly and that last member is needed in the fray).

"LEVEL" WEAK PARTY MEMBERS

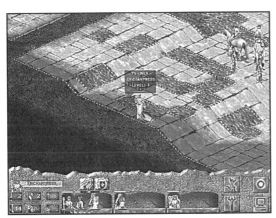

Fig. 4-2. This Mage will be worthless in the upcoming battle, but she still will gain experience points as a result of the victory.

An important trick in combat is the process of "leveling" fresh recruits. This process involves taking units that aren't particularly combat-worthy—due to their low level—and attaching them to a big, powerful army, as shown in figure 4-2. These units should not participate in combat directly, but should stand off to the side and watch the proceedings. This keeps them safe.

As the army gains experience, so do its weakest members. Since experience is doled out more or less equally to each surviving party member, actual individual performance in combat doesn't matter in the least.

After a few victories, your weak party members will have gained sufficient levels to make a real contribution in battle. At this point, they can either start participating directly in battles or leave the army to pursue other tasks.

> Although you can use this "leveling" trick with any type of unit, you will find that Mages almost ALWAYS have to be leveled in this way.

OVERVIEW OF COMBAT

Combat may be broken down into several distinct (if somewhat arbitrary) phases. Thinking about combat in terms of phases often helps when you try to plan and execute a specific strategy.

STARTING PHASE

The starting phase begins when combat itself begins, and it continues until one side makes a definite move to attack.

Combat always starts out paused in single-player games of **Lords of Magic.** Don't immediately set the battle in motion, unless your forces so thoroughly outnumber or outclass the enemy that you have little to fear.

PLOT INITIAL MOVEMENTS

Your forces rarely start out in a good combat formation. Take this opportunity to issue orders while the game is paused. Position your melee units between the enemy and your more fragile missile troops and Mages, or move the missile troops and Mages back to a safer distance.

It's usually a good idea to amass all or most of your melee attackers into a single mob. If you plan to use a few melee troops to flank the enemy, you can send them on their way immediately.

If you plan to move your entire army, you may want to do that at this time. If your army features lots of missile troops and you begin on rocky ground, for example, you may want to move everyone to a flatter area where your missile units will have a chance to see the enemy.

Even if your plan is to charge in and attack the enemy, you should still take this opportunity to get your army into a good combat position (melee troops in front, others in back).

LAUNCH A SPELL

If spells are part of your battle strategy, you may also want to initiate a spell before setting the battle in motion. Some spells have short durations and require precise timing, but many spells last long enough that you can cast them at the beginning of the battle without worrying about their effects wearing off. Other spells, such as Lightning and other damage-dealing spells, have instant effects and may be cast at any time. Casting these spells immediately is usually a good strategy.

Fig. 4-3. Cast your direct-damage spells early. This lets you finish off enemies before they can cause any damage in return. (Note the enemy getting blasted by a Spirit Arrow.)

EARLY ATTACK PHASE

As you set the battle in motion, you need to bear in mind what sort of strategy you wish to pursue. Do you want to hang back and defend a piece of land, or charge in and smash the enemy as quickly as possible? Perhaps you want to do a bit of both. All these strategies are viable, though some are easier to execute than others.

DEFENSIVE STRATEGIES

A defensive strategy is usually easier to execute properly than an offensive one. If you intend to sit back and wait, you have ample time to amass your melee troops, position your missile troops for good shots, and have your Mages prepare a few lethal spells.

Defense is even easier if you choose a suitable location. If your army has considerable missile troops, you may want to camp on a broad flat area where these troops can shoot enemies from a distance. Establishing a position on high ground also works well because the enemy will have to climb the slope to reach you. This slows enemy units down, allowing your missile troops to get in more shots. Also, your position on high ground sometimes affects the enemy's melee troops' ability to attack in a large group; these troops tend to slow down and split up as they charge at you. The end result is that they reach the point of attack one by one instead of in a big powerful group.

The computer opponent often breaks a few units away from its main army to flank you; it's important to watch for this. Keep a few melee troops in reserve, so that they may intercept flankers before they reach your valuable missile troops and Mages.

Defensive strategies are recommended for most battles. Figure 4-4 illustrates a good general-purpose formation for defense.

Fig. 4-4. This is a typical formation: melee troops are in a mob at the front; missile troops are somewhat to the rear; and Mages are the farthest back.

ATTACK STRATEGIES

Wild attacks are seldom a great idea, especially against the computer. Your missile troops have less time to plant their feet and fire when you force them to charge in. Also, there's always the problem of keeping your army together when it's moving. If you are having real difficulty, you can pause the game frequently to make minor adjustments and to keep units on track, but you still will run into problems when you send troops across narrow or difficult patches of terrain.

Feel free to attack in the formation shown in figure 4-4. Another good attack formation is shown in figure 4-5.

Fig. 4-5. This attack formation has your melee troops in two separate but relatively close groups. In an attack, these two groups converge in a "pincers" movement, encircling enemy units and subjecting them to injury from two different directions.

Ideally, several of your men should always be able to reach the target and should begin striking simultaneously. This ideal isn't always possible, but by frequently pausing combat and having your men approach as a large group, you can often come close.

You should attack if enemy units get thoroughly split up. Split-up enemy units usually try to time their attacks so that they all reach your army at the same time from different directions. By moving your entire army to crush individual enemy bands, you take advantage of the enemy's lack of cohesiveness and disrupt its timing.

COMBINED STRATEGIES

Even if you adopt a purely defensive strategy, you should consider sending a few flankers into the fray. The classic trick is to send cavalry off to one side of the enemy army. Then have them loop in from the side or back to pummel enemy Mages or missile troops while all the other troops are busy fighting one another. Figure 4-6 illustrates this maneuver.

This technique is highly recommended if your opponent has missile troops in his army.

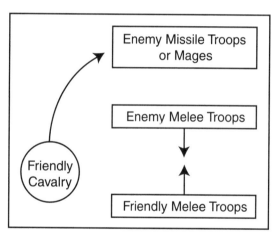

Fig. 4-6. Use cavalry flankers to sneak past enemy melee troops to attack fragile Mages or missile troops directly.

MELEE

Once both armies' melee troops clash, it's up to you to influence the battle as best you can. Position missile troops so that they may pick away at enemy forces, and have Mages cast timely spells that may sway the fortunes of battle.

Continually assign both your melee and missile troops new targets. A troop tends to become confused or simply waits for orders after killing its current target. Also, be sure not to give them awkward or unreachable targets. If you assign them to an enemy at the back of the enemy army, your men will obediently wade through the enemy to reach their target(s). But they usually get cut down in the process! Instead, you should have your troops attack targets at the forefront of the enemy formation.

Don't be afraid to retreat. Send damaged units to the rear of your army, and have **any** troops in a bad spot retreat to more favorable ground. Retreating often buys extra time for your missile troops to do their work.

VICTORY OR FLIGHT

Finally, the battle ends—either in the annihilation or in the flight of one side. Cast the appropriate spells on the dead and exit to gloat over the spoils.

COMBAT SUBTLETIES

You can succeed in combat with only the basic knowledge we have covered thus far in this chapter. You can also refine and improve your combat skills if you understand advanced options and when to use them. Here's a list of useful tips and tricks.

UNDERSTANDING TERRAIN

In combat, terrain is significant in the following ways:

- Steep inclines slow units down, making them vulnerable to missile attacks. Inclines also make it difficult for an army to maintain its formation. Avoid crossing this type of terrain when the enemy is within attack range.

- Broad plains allow freedom to flank and maneuver; while narrow, enclosed areas force units to attack in one of several "paths." The former terrain favors missile attacks and flanking, while the latter forces head-on combat.

- Certain rough spots are hard for walking units to access, but they can easily be crossed by flying units. Use this to your advantage, placing flying troops—such as Fae Slingers—in areas where they're extremely hard to reach by foot.

Understand the effects of terrain, and you'll be much more efficient in battle.

PAUSING COMBAT

You can pause combat as frequently as you want, and you can give units detailed orders while the game is on pause. Many players won't be accustomed to this unusual feature; hence, there's always the chance that it won't be used at all.

If you find yourself getting swamped, or the battle isn't going quite the way you had expected, or you're wondering what has become of an enemy flanking party that you can't see on screen—just pause the game and address the problem. Similarly, if your melee troops have killed their target, and you aren't sure whether they'll attack the nearest enemy or just wait for orders, pause the game and give them new orders immediately. With the ability to pause the game at any time, you should never feel as though things are out of control. (Figure 4-7 shows an intense melee, which has been paused to allow for greater tactical control.)

Fig. 4-7. Fighting tough enemies requires you to use every advantage at your disposal. Pausing the game is an important tool!

In particular, Mages can benefit greatly from pausing the game. A typical spellcasting strategy is to pause the game, order a Mage to cast a spell, and "un-pause" the game. As the spell leaves the Mage's fingertips, pause the game again and order him to cast another spell. Repeat as necessary.

This technique allows your Mage to cast several spells before the enemy gets anywhere near your troops. This tactic is particularly useful when your Mage casts damaging spells; it lets him kill enemy units well before the main phase of combat begins.

ADVANCED ATTACK OPTIONS

Here are a few tips on using advanced combat options. This section doesn't cover every option available to you (see the manual for that), but it does clarify situations in which you should exercise these options.

BERSERK

Melee troops ordered to go Berserk will see their Defense drop to zero and their Attack increase by half of their original Defense.

Use this command when the enemy outclasses your army or when your puny Warriors try to hack apart a big, tough enemy but cause little damage due to their meager Attack ratings. Never use this command when you charge at enemy missile troops, as Berserk makes your men much more vulnerable to missiles.

AIMED ATTACK

Aimed Attack increases missile attack damage by half but greatly increases the time required to aim and fire.

As with Berserk, you should use Aimed Attacks against tough enemies that aren't sustaining too much damage from your troops' projectiles. In other situations, a normal attack is usually preferable.

PARRY

Parry reduces a unit's Attack but increases Defense by one-quarter of the original Attack value.

This is a good setting for melee troops that are simply trying to hold their own. For example, you can have your melee troops Parry to hold their ground while missile troops or Mages unleash most of the damage against enemy units.

> Use the Parry setting on melee troops when your army includes many potent missile troops or Mages, and when you're concerned that the enemy will break through and reach your missile troops or Mages before they can do their job.

SUBDUE ATTACK

Thieves can attempt to Subdue enemy Champions instead of killing them; a Subdue Attack allows them to take prisoners.

Use the Subdue Attack when you have whittled enemy opposition down to almost nothing, and you have used regular attacks to decrease the target Champion's health to a dangerous level. If you try to use a Subdue Attack on a healthy Champion with a full army around him, you frequently will lose the battle. The healthy enemy cheerfully hacks your men to bits as they try to Subdue the Champion instead of fighting him properly!

HIDE AND RALLY

Hiding can lead to devastating flank attacks, while Rally fractionally increases nearby troops' combat abilities. What do these abilities have in common? They offer potential benefits for **free!** Use them whenever possible—they don't have any drawbacks.

MOB ATTACKS

In most infantry or cavalry battles, your main goal is to keep your melee troops together in a huge mob. Why? Since enemies are temporarily incapacitated when they are hit, an enemy that is hit multiple times in rapid succession is virtually paralyzed and cannot fight back. Mobs allow your troops to get in multiple attacks on individual enemies, virtually paralyzing them in this fashion.

On the other hand, letting your troops fight individually makes them vulnerable to enemy mob attacks. Only use individuals or small groups of melee attackers to eliminate vulnerable missile troops or Mages.

> **Your infantry mob should be roughly linear instead of being a true mob without shape. Attacking in a long line formation allows as many of your melee troops as possible to start attacking the enemy immediately.**
>
> **Conversely, a circular mob places many of your melee troops at the rear of the formation, unable to bring their weapons to bear on the enemy.**

GROUPED MISSILE FIRE

Have all your missile troops target a single unit (see figure 4-8). This tactic works the same way as a mob attack works: If enough missile troops target

Fig. 4-8. These Fae Slingers all cast their rocks at a single foe. This target is virtually immobilized by the rain of rocks.

a single unit, they can virtually immobilize the enemy unit with their repeated missiles, forcing it to stand in place until it collapses.

PRELIMINARY ATTACKS

If an enemy army is too tough for your army, send in a wave of "shock troops" first, which can be a group of freshly hired mercenaries. The shock troops' only goal is to attack the enemy army in order to weaken it somewhat before your main army enters the fray.

Freshly hired mercenaries usually can't hurt a tough opponent with direct attacks. If you load up on fast cavalry mercenaries, you can, however, have several of them try to flank the enemy, picking away at fragile missile attackers and spellcasters. At the very least, the enemy spellcasters will deplete their mana in this battle, leaving them vulnerable if your main army attacks during the same turn as the shock troops.

> For reasons explained later in this chapter, do not use Auto Calculate when you attack with shock troops.

AUTO CALCULATE

The Auto Calculate option resolves battle instantaneously. It tends to be fairly lenient, and it produces better results than you could get by fighting the battle manually.

Auto Calculated combats tend to be all-or-nothing affairs. One side tends to lose everything, while the other is only marginally injured. Auto Calculate, therefore, is a great way to resolve battles quickly where your army is somewhat superior to that of the enemy. Chances are good that pressing the Auto Calculate button will yield you a quick, painless victory.

Since Auto Calculate does tend to produce all-or-nothing results, you shouldn't use it when your men are hopelessly outclassed; for example, when your weak mercenary shock troops are just trying to cause a little damage to a superior enemy army. In these cases, you can usually cause more damage by fighting manually and using clever flanking tactics to pick apart enemy missile troops and Mages.

FINAL COMBAT NOTES

As stated at this chapter's beginning, you'll find combat in **Lords of Magic** to be a relatively simple affair. Armies with a strong complement of melee troops, a few missile troops, and a few Mages tend to be the strongest. Experience is very important; battles between veterans and green troops almost always favor the veterans. Dense formations and mob attacks tend to rule the day, while stragglers are usually cut down with the greatest of ease. Remember these rules and you'll have a distinct advantage on the battlefield.

> Chapter 6 covers advanced tips on LORDS OF MAGIC and includes detailed comparisons of each Faith's units. Refer to this chapter for more information on which units are best for your individual combat strategy.

> Magic is the strongest weapon in the later stages of the game.

MAGIC

The following compendium lists every spell in the game and includes tips on using each spell effectively. Spells are sorted by faith; within each faith, they're further organized by spell book and then by power.

Several types of information are given for each spell. Aside from the spell name, you'll find the following entries:

- Mana Cost tells you how many mana points are needed to cast a particular spell successfully.

- Research Cost lets you see how many man-hours are required to research the spell.

- Spell Type tells you whether this spell is used in the Combat screen, on the World Map, or with both.

- Target lists what you can cast a particular spell on; armies, locations, and individual units are all possible targets.

Spells are listed in the order in which you must research them. For example, within the Attack spell book of the Air faith, it's necessary to have researched Headwind and Lightning before researching Poison Cloud.

> One of the most fun and exciting parts of Lords of Magic is finding combinations of spells that work well together. Keep your eyes open for spells that can be used effectively in combinations!

AIR SPELLS

Air spells feature a good mix of offense and defense. Many Air spells affect the speed of a target unit, either positively or negatively. These spells may not seem too powerful on first inspection, but you can use them in any number of clever ways. Spend some time thinking about the possibilities for these spells, and you'll be surprised by what you come up with.

Fig. 5-1. This diagram illustrates Air's research hierarchy.

ATTACK	DEFENSE	GENERAL	OVERLAND
Head Wind	Swiftness	Teleport Artifact	Wind Walk
Lightning Bolt	Essence of the Wisp	Dispel Magic	Wind Mills
Poison Cloud	Guardian Winds	Ether Gauze	Sand Storm
Cone of Cold	Cloud of War	Seer	Ice
Stun	Lightning Charge	Detect Earth	
Chain Lightning			

ATTACK SPELL BOOK

HEADWIND

Mana Cost: 2

Research Cost: 10

Spell Type: Combat

Target: Single Unit

Headwind greatly reduces the target's ability to move and attack in combat. The spell's duration is unaffected by the caster's level, so it's a good spell for low-level Mages.

This is a very powerful spell despite its low cost and seemingly unimpressive effect. By slowing down enemy units with Headwind, you buy time, giving your missile troops more chances to shoot. You can also split up groups of attackers by slowing down one or more of them, making them late for battle. Also, you can use Headwind to give other spells a chance to work. Cast Headwind on a unit that's already been hit with a Poison Cloud spell, and the Poison Cloud gets more time to work.

LIGHTNING

Mana Cost: 2

Research Cost: 10

Spell Type: Combat

Target: Single Unit

Lightning deals damage equal to three plus one half of the caster's level against a single target. If the caster is Level 4, for example, Lightning deals damage with a base of five—3 + 1/2 of 4.

This is a basic direct-damage spell. Spells like these are best against missile troops and enemy spellcasters, which have relatively low toughness. These units can be dispatched with only a few direct-damage spells.

POISON CLOUD

Mana Cost: 4
Research Cost: 100
Spell Type: Combat
Target: Single Unit

Poison Cloud has a lingering effect that deals two points of damage to its target every four seconds for a maximum of 20 damage points. The spell ends when 20 points have been dealt.

Poison Cloud works best on units that are slow or far from your own troops because the Cloud needs time to act. Headwind is a great way to slow down units afflicted with Poison Cloud; it forces them to sit and take their damage.

CONE OF COLD

Mana Cost: 8
Research Cost: 151
Spell Type: Combat
Target: Area

Cone of Cold targets a single unit, but anything caught within its radius is damaged to the tune of three plus one third of the caster's level in damage. The spell's radius varies according to the caster's level.

This sort of spell works best when it targets a unit in a crowd. If you use it on an individual enemy standing by himself, you're wasting mana. Use Lightning in these cases!

STUN

Mana Cost: 8

Research Cost: 175

Spell Type: Combat

Target: Single Unit

Stun freezes an enemy in place, so that it can neither move nor attack for the duration of the spell. The spell's duration depends on the caster's level. The only hitch is that the caster must be at least two levels higher than the target, or the spell will not work.

Stun is a great way to immobilize enemies, rendering them completely helpless. It's best used against an opposing force that includes one big tough unit (which can be Stunned) and a bunch of smaller units. It's least useful when you're facing hordes of small units because Stunning just one of these units won't make much of a difference.

CHAIN LIGHTNING

Mana Cost: 10

Research Cost: 220

Spell Type: Combat

Target: Multiple Units

Chain Lightning targets a single unit, but any unit caught in the spell's area of effect suffers damage points equal to three plus one half of the caster's level, as the multiple bolts strike each target.

Again, this sort of spell works best when it targets a unit in a crowd. If you use it on individual enemies standing by themselves, you're wasting mana.

DEFENSE SPELL BOOK

SWIFTNESS

Mana Cost: 2

Research Cost: 10

Spell Type: Combat

Target: Single Unit

Swiftness increases a single unit's speed in combat. The spell's duration varies according to the caster's level.

Swiftness is a good spell to cast on both melee and missile troops. Swiftness-affected troops strike and recover faster; hence, they are much more effective than their slower counterparts.

ESSENCE OF THE WISP

Mana Cost: 2

Research Cost: 12

Spell Type: Combat

Target: Single Unit

Essence of the Wisp causes a unit to float above the ground, thereby conferring 25 percent resistance to Earth magic. The spell's duration is unaffected by the caster's level.

This highly specialized spell is a great asset if you happen to be fighting Earth units. Cast it on all your units whenever you're battling Earth's Mages!

GUARDIAN WINDS

Mana Cost: 4

Research Cost: 43

Spell Type: Combat

Target: Single Unit

Guardian Winds bestows 50 percent missile resistance upon the target for a fixed amount of time.

This is the sort of spell that can be a real lifesaver—or completely useless; it all depends on how many missile troops your army faces. A favorite tactic is to cast this spell on your cavalry units before they rush in to attack the enemy's missile troops. This prevents the cavalry from being shot full of arrows as they approach the enemy.

Another favorite target of this spell is your leader. A Lord is always a prime target for rocks and arrows, and this spell helps cut down on those cheap shots.

CLOUD OF WAR

Mana Cost: 4

Research Cost: 81

Spell Type: Combat

Target: Single Unit

Cloud of War bestows +3 Defense upon its target for a limited time.

This is a straightforward spell with a useful effect. A bonus of three Defense automatically translates into three Defense points for the targeted unit.

Melee units are usually the best recipients of this spell. Missile troops tend to be overwhelmed if the enemy gets too close, regardless of how much extra Defense you give them. Melee units, on the other hand, really benefit from this extra edge.

LIGHTNING CHARGE

Mana Cost: 8

Research Cost: 164

Spell Type: Combat

Target: Single Unit

Lightning Charge bestows +3 to the target unit's Attack rating. Furthermore, if an enemy strikes the unit, the enemy receives damage equal to three plus one third of the caster's level.

This is an interesting spell because it creates two distinct effects, both of which can be extremely helpful. Cast this spell on front-line melee attackers to provide an extra punch at the point of attack.

GENERAL SPELL BOOK

TELEPORT ARTIFACT

Mana Cost: 2

Research Cost: 15

Spell Type: World Map

Target: Single Artifact

Teleport Artifact surveys all friendly cities and teleports the Mage's unassigned artifacts to a friendly unit (if found). If no units are found, the spell looks for friendly units in a structure, such as a Barracks. If no appropriate units are found there, the spell fails, and the caster keeps his artifacts.

This spell is extremely useful for late-game artifact distribution. Without it, your main army tends to get bogged down in the logistics of getting artifacts into the hands of capable owners.

DISPEL MAGIC

Mana Cost: 4

Research Cost: 42

Spell Type: Both

Target: Enchantment

Dispel Magic is used to cancel other Mages' spells. If the level of the caster of Dispel Magic is greater than that of the Mage whose enchantment is being dispelled, Dispel Magic automatically works. If not, Dispel Magic fails.

Dispel Magic is ideal for getting rid of any non-instantaneous enemy spell, such as a pesky Poison Cloud or Golgotha's Gift.

ETHER GAUZE

Mana Cost: 4

Research Cost: 59

Spell Type: World Map

Target: Party

Ether Gauze causes a party to regain Hit Points at an increased rate of +1 per turn when the party is stationary; the effect lasts for three turns.

Spells, such as Ether Gauze, are particularly useful when it isn't feasible to heal your army at a Capital's Temple.

SEER

Mana Cost: 4

Research Cost: 90

Spell Type: World Map

Target: Location

Seer reveals the terrain of a selected location, along with any Chaos, Death, or Fire units in the vicinity.

Every faith has a spell like this, which reveals the location of several of its traditional enemies. These spells are useful for planning attacks and figuring out what the bad guys are up to.

DETECT EARTH

Mana Cost: 8

Research Cost: 50

Spell Type: World Map

Target: Caster

The location of any Earth units within a certain radius of the caster (10 map units) are revealed. Earth is a traditional enemy of Air.

OVERLAND SPELL BOOK

WINDWALK

Mana Cost: 2

Research Cost: 7

Spell Type: World Map

Target: Party

Windwalk temporarily increases a party's overland travel speed by 25 percent.

Cast this spell on any turn that your Mages aren't likely to enter combat. Since mana is fully regenerated every turn, you'll make the most of a resource that would otherwise be wasted.

WIND MILLS

Mana Cost: 4

Research Cost: 45

Spell Type: World Map

Target: Capital

Wind Mills boosts ale production in the targeted Capital by +1.

A bonus of one ale may initially seem like a trivial amount, but when it's cast on each of your cities, the spell's effects can add up.

SAND STORM

Mana Cost: 4

Research Cost: 122

Spell Type: World Map

Target: Party

Sand Storm temporarily reduces the target party's movement points by three and deals two plus one half of the caster's level in damage points.

This spell is a good way to "freeze" a rampaging army intent on attacking you. It not only slows the charge, thus giving you more time to prepare, but also deals a modicum of damage. Cast it multiple times while you flee from the army you're targeting. Then, reverse course and attack. If all goes well, the enemy will be so weakened that your victory is practically automatic.

ICE

Mana Cost: 4

Research Cost: 135

Spell Type: World Map

Target: Location

This spell turns a target location into tundra, Air's native terrain.

Air units travel marginally faster on tundra. Constant application of this spell can turn large patches of terrain into Air-friendly havens, giving Air units sort of a "home-court advantage" even away from home.

CHAOS SPELLS

The overriding principle of Chaos spells is randomness. If you like to be sure what you're getting when you cast a spell, you'll hate Chaos—but if you like a surprise, you'll love this batch of spells. Many of these spells are more potent than other faiths' comparable spells if they work properly. That's a big if! You'll need nerves of steel and lots of patience when you cast Chaos spells—you'll just never know what the end result will be.

5-2. Here's the research hierarchy for Chaos spells.

ATTACK	DEFENSE	GENERAL	OVERLAND
Blind Rage	Crash	Teleport Artifact	Minor Fate
Blades of Fury	Blink	Dispel Magic	Invoke Fate
Wheel of Fortune	Shimmering Veil	Tourniquet	Wanderlust
Hand of Fate	Polymorph Self	Detect Order	Winds of Change
Confusion			Reincarnation
Vortex			
Polymorph Other			

Attack Spell Book

Blind Rage

Mana Cost: 2

Research Cost: 26

Spell Type: Combat

Target: Single Unit

If the caster is at least two levels higher than the target, the target rushes uncontrollably toward the caster with murderous intent.

Initially, this may sound like a useless spell, but after some thought, its uses become apparent. Cast it on enemy missile troops and spellcasters to make them abandon their position and charge in recklessly. At that point, your waiting melee troops can cut them to bits.

You can also break up groups of melee units by casting this spell on one or two group members. Mob attacks are very effective in **Lords of Magic**, and you'll find this technique useful for breaking up enemy mobs and for catching fleeing enemies.

Wheel of Fortune

Mana Cost: 4

Research Cost: 62

Spell Type: Combat

Target: Single Unit

Wheel of Fortune causes variable changes in the target unit's combat statistics. These changes can be positive or negative.

This spell poses more questions than answers. Should you cast it on friend or against foe? At the start or end of combat? It's up to you to come up with your own answers to this difficult dilemma.

Here's a good way to start: cast this spell on one of your weaker combat units. If the results are bad, cast it again. By targeting one of your weakest units, you have little to lose (the weak unit may become weaker, but so what!) and much to gain (the unit may actually become capable). Or cast it on the very toughest enemy you can find, especially in battles where you have a good chance of losing. In these cases, you'll probably get torched anyway. In this case, you may as well alter the enemy's best unit and hope the changes are for the worse!

HAND OF FATE

Mana Cost: 4
Research Cost: 120
Spell Type: Combat
Target: Single Unit

This spell has a 60 percent chance (plus 3 percent for every level of the caster) of causing twice the caster's level in damage to the target. If the spell fails, however, the caster takes the damage.

This is another risky spell. When it works properly, it deals much more damage than comparable spells at comparable mana costs. But when it backfires…it really hurts.

Do the math before casting this spell. If the spellcaster can withstand the damage caused by a backfire, feel free to cast it. Of course, you should also feel free to cast it in desperate situations, regardless of the consequences. And if you manage to find an artifact that bestows partial immunity to the effects of Chaos, you can use this spell with reckless abandon and suffer only a fraction of the normal consequences!

BLADES OF FURY

Mana Cost: 6

Research Cost: 192

Spell Type: Chaos

Target: Single Unit

This spell causes spinning blades to appear and fly out from the caster. These blades circle and deal three points of damage every time they touch a unit. The blades move at random in a circle.

Here's yet another random spell for you to ponder. These blades can tear up an enemy army—if they can just manage to get close enough. This spell targets a unit. Place your scout where you would like your blades to be. Wish the poor guy well.

CONFUSION

Mana Cost: 6

Research Cost: 135

Spell Type: Combat

Target: Single Unit

If the caster's level is at least two greater than the target's level, the target is confused and attacks anyone nearby—even friendly units.

This spell's best target is an enemy in a group. This way, Confusion causes him to attack one of his friends. If you cast this spell on a unit that's already fighting your men, you aren't likely to affect that unit's behavior much with this spell.

Always be on the lookout for units that could be particularly devastating when confused. A melee unit standing right next to a group of missile troops, for example, could cause all sorts of damage if Confused.

VORTEX

Mana Cost: 10

Research Cost: 150

Spell Type: Combat

Target: Multiple Units

A Vortex appears and targets all units within a radius determined by the caster's level. The Vortex moves at random in a circular motion and causes one point of damage every time it touches a unit.

Again, this is a spell that can be dangerous or incredibly effective, depending partially on fate. Cast it in the middle of a group of enemies so that you'll be assured of dealing some damage from the very start.

This is a good spell to use when you have extremely fast units on your side, as speed helps units avoid the Vortex.

POLYMORPH OTHER

Mana Cost: 12

Research Cost: 192

Spell Type: Combat

Target: Single Unit

The target unit is transformed into a completely random creature (type).

As with any spell that has a completely random effect, it's recommended that you cast this spell on a very strong unit of the enemy. This is an extremely potent spell if you pick your targets properly.

Defense Spell Book

Crash

Mana Cost: 2
Research Cost: 13
Spell Type: Combat
Target: Single Unit

This spell's target takes a random amount of damage and loses three Hit Points permanently; however, it gains a temporary, random increase in combat stats.

This spell is fairly devastating to units with low Hit Points and will seriously weaken any unit with repeated castings. It's advisable, therefore, to cast this spell primarily on mercenaries. This way your loyal troops won't be injured by the spell's serious downside. Note that this spell can be a real life-saver if the battle is going against you.

Blink

Mana Cost: 4
Research Cost: 13
Spell Type: Combat
Target: Caster

The caster is teleported to a different spot on the battlefield for 10 seconds, after which point he or she is returned to the original spot.

This is a good spell for escaping difficult situations. Don't cast it if your Mage is in a good spot already, as you just may teleport him into trouble!

SHIMMERING VEIL

Mana Cost: 4
Research Cost: 129
Spell Type: Combat
Target: Single Unit

The targeted unit gains temporary 50 percent missile resistance and +2 Defense.

Shimmering Veil is one of very few Chaos spells that bestows a permanent, non-variable benefit. This spell is particularly useful for Mages, front-line troops, or anyone that stands a good chance of being pelted by enemy missile troops.

POLYMORPH SELF

Mana Cost: 12
Research Cost: 192
Spell Type: Combat
Target: Caster

The caster is changed into a random creature type based on his level.

This spell is always a gamble because any caster whose level is actually high enough to cast this spell isn't worth losing. There's nothing, however, that says your spellcaster can't just run away or hide if he's transformed into a fragile creature.

Cast Polymorph Self near the start of combat, while the enemy is still distant. Then figure out what to do with the spellcaster based on what he has turned into. Note that if you are polymorphed into a chicken, cow, goat, or elephant the effect is permanent until dispelled.

GENERAL SPELL BOOK

TELEPORT ARTIFACT

Mana Cost: 2

Research Cost: 22

Spell Type: World Map

Target: Artifact

As with other Teleport Artifact spells, this spell searches friendly Capitals for a unit capable of receiving the caster's unassigned artifacts. If found, the artifacts are transferred to that unit. If not found, friendly structures, such as Barracks, are searched. If no suitable units are found in either Capitals or outlying structures, the caster retains his artifacts.

DISPEL MAGIC

Mana Cost: 2

Research Cost: 42

Spell Type: Both

Target: Enchantment

Dispel Magic targets any existing spell. If the caster's level is greater than that of the caster who generated the targeted spell, the targeted spell is negated.

TOURNIQUET

Mana Cost: 4

Research Cost: 45

Spell Type: World Map

Target: Party

The targeted party gains +2 Hit Points per turn when it does not move during the next three turns.

This spell is more powerful than similar spells possessed by other faiths. For example, Air's Ether Gauze only recovers one extra Hit Point per turn.

DETECT ORDER

Mana Cost: 4

Research Cost: 50

Spell Type: World Map

Target: Area

The locations of any Order units within 10 tiles of the caster are revealed.

REINCARNATION

Mana Cost: 12

Research Cost: 192

Spell Type: Combat

Target: Single Unit

The targeted dead unit is raised as a random type of unit of its original faith.

Since the unit you're targeting is already dead, you hardly can lose anything by Reincarnating it.

This is a great spell, especially in battles that you're fairly sure you can win. In these winnable battles, it doesn't matter too much if you spend all your mana on Reincarnate—it doesn't produce anything useful. But if you do produce a powerful unit, you'll be able to integrate that unit into your army.

OVERLAND SPELL BOOK

MINOR FATE

Mana Cost: 2

Research Cost: 20

Spell Type: World Map

Target: Party

Minor Fate causes temporary gains or losses of combat statistics in the affected party. The degree of change depends on the spellcaster's level.

Again, this is another spell that could hurt or heal. Cast it on weak stacks of friendly units or against tough stacks of enemies—or, do the reverse. It's all up to chance!

INVOKE FATE

Mana Cost: 4

Research Cost: 45

Spell Type: World Map

Target: Capital

The targeted Capital has a permanent +1 gain in resource production. The type of resource affected is random; it's determined as the spell is cast.

WANDERLUST

Mana Cost: 4

Research Cost: 63

Spell Type: World Map

Target: Party

The targeted party gains a temporary increase at +15 percent to +35 percent in overland movement.

This is a typical movement-enhancing spell, but with Chaos's trademark randomness built into it. Cast it frequently when your Mages have little else to do.

WINDS OF CHANGE

Mana Cost: 8

Research Cost: 110

Spell Type: World Map

Target: Location

The targeted area's terrain is converted to a random terrain type.

This is an amusing spell, but it's somewhat less useful than the terrain-affecting spells of the other faiths. Since the end result is a terrain type randomly determined (and not necessarily of Chaos's home turf), the spell doesn't necessarily confer any benefits on Chaos parties traveling across the affected terrain.

DEATH SPELLS

The Death spell book includes a wide variety of direct-damage spells and, thus, provides several options for Mages who look to wreak havoc on the enemy. The book also includes spells that allow you to summon creatures directly into combat—as opposed to summoning them in Mages' Towers—and to raise the dead as Zombies on a temporary basis. Since summoned creatures last beyond combat itself, Death's spell book produces potent, permanent armies more cheaply than any other faith can.

Fig. 5-3. This is the research hierarchy for Death spells.

ATTACK	DEFENSE	GENERAL	OVERLAND
Curse	Unholy Word	Dispel Magic	Funeral March
Balkoth's Word	Visage of Horror	Detect Life	Raise Skeleton
Primal Fear	Embrace of Golgotha	Purge Wounds	Spawn Cave
Golgotha's Gift	Walk Among Us	Teleport Artifact	Locust Swarm
Decay			Pestilence
Dark Shadows			Raise Shade
Lost Soul			

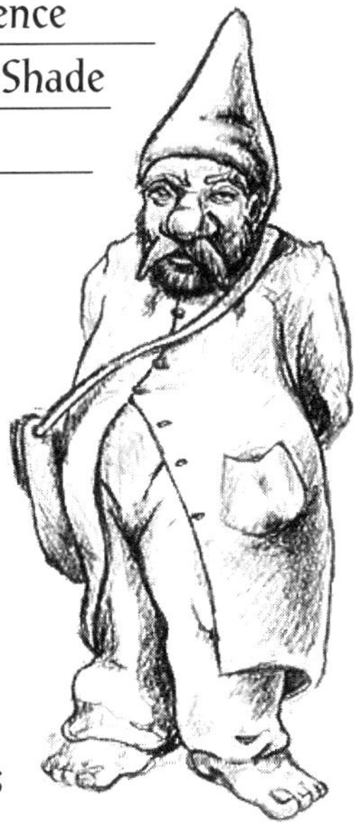

ATTACK SPELL BOOK

CURSE

Mana Cost: 2

Research Cost: 5

Spell Type: Combat

Target: Single Unit

Curse damages the target unit by an amount equal to three plus one half of the caster's level.

This is a typical direct-damage spell, much like Air's Lightning. Use it to annihilate weak units or chip away at tough ones.

BALKOTH'S WORD

Mana Cost: 4
Research Cost: 21
Spell Type: Combat
Target: Single Unit

Balkoth's Word damages the targeted unit by an amount equal to six plus one half of the caster's level, provided that the caster is at least one level higher than the intended target.

This spell is much more potent that the typical direct-damage spell, but bear in mind that two Curse spells cost the same as a single Balkoth's Word and deal comparable damage. Thus, in some ways, Curse is the superior spell.

PRIMAL FEAR

Mana Cost: 4
Research Cost: 34
Spell Type: Combat
Target: Area

Primal Fear targets all enemies within a short radius (four map units) of the caster. All targeted units less than the eighth level suffer a temporary −4 to both Strength and Dexterity.

The only real downside to this spell is that it requires the caster to get close to the action. Use careful unit placement to ensure that your melee troops protect your Mage at all times.

GOLGOTHA'S GIFT

Mana Cost: 6
Research Cost: 81
Spell Type: Combat
Target: Single Unit

When Golgotha's Gift is cast, it deals one point of damage to, and infects, the target unit. Any unit grouped with an infected unit also becomes infected, provided that it's of a lower level than Golgotha's Gift's caster. All infected units' ability to heal is impaired by –3 per turn. The infection can be removed by visiting a Capital's Temple, not a Great Temple.

The net effect of Golgotha's Gift is that targeted units cannot be healed through normal means. It's more of a nuisance than anything to have to go to the Temple to be healed. This spell is also a good way to ensure that an injured army doesn't get back into fighting shape anytime soon.

DECAY

Mana Cost: 8
Research Cost: 93
Spell Type: Combat
Target: Single Unit

Decay inflicts the target unit with one point of damage every three seconds for a maximum of 20 points of damage.

This type of spell works best on slow units or units away from combat. Slowness and distance give the spell time to take effect.

DARK SHADOWS

Mana Cost: 8
Research Cost: 148
Spell Type: Combat
Target: Single Unit

Dark Shadows deals damage to the target unit equal to twice the caster's level minus the target unit's level.

This is one of the more powerful direct-damage spells in the game, especially when cast by a high-level Mage on a lower-level target. If you have a choice between Curse and Dark Shadows, however, you should do the math mentally to figure out which can cause more damage in a particular instance. Remember that, in terms of mana, you can cast four Curses for every Dark Shadows!

LOST SOUL

Mana Cost: 12
Research Cost: 192
Spell Type: Combat
Target: Single Unit

Lost Soul summons a ghostlike Lost Soul that pursues the targeted unit. The target unit dies if the lost soul comes in contact with it.

This is an all-or-nothing spell that either kills the target outright or misses completely. Use it on the most powerful enemies, as its high casting cost is too much to waste on lesser foes.

DEFENSE SPELL BOOK

UNHOLY WORD

Mana Cost: 2

Research Cost: 3

Spell Type: Combat

Target: Single Unit

Unholy Word temporarily increases the target unit's Attack rating by two.

This is a cheap spell with a simple effect. Use it frequently when your Mages are at low-levels; melee units are the best targets.

VISAGE OF HORROR

Mana Cost: 4

Research Cost: 4

Spell Type: Combat

Target: All Units

Visage of Horror causes all Death units to gain, temporarily, two Attack and one Defense. (Ranged Attack is only increased by one.) In addition, all non-Death units receive −1 for their Defenses.

This spell is superior to Unholy Word, especially if your army consists of more than two units. Its effectiveness is diluted somewhat if your army has any non-Death units.

EMBRACE OF GOLGOTHA

Mana Cost: 6

Research Cost: 112

Spell Type: Combat

Target: Single Friendly Unit

Embrace of Golgotha kills a friendly unit. The caster then gains a number of mana points equal to the target unit's Hit Points, possibly raising the caster's mana above his normal maximum.

This spell requires a great sacrifice and is only useful in epic battles where your spellcaster knows spells capable of altering the face of battle. If your Mage truly does not have any great spells to cast, Embrace of Golgotha is a waste of a unit.

If you intend to use this spell, be sure to cast it before your Mage's mana points run dry. Despite the fact that the spell creates mana, it costs a good deal of mana to cast.

Finally, bear in mind that you must sacrifice a unit with high Hit Points to make this spell pay off. If you target a friendly scout unit with only five Hit Points, for example, your Mage actually loses mana by casting this spell because the spell costs six mana to cast. In this case, the Mage only receives five mana in return for his effort (a net loss of one mana).

WALK AMONG US

Mana Cost: 10

Research Cost: 135

Spell Type: Combat

Target: Single Dead Unit

The targeted unit is raised as a Zombie. This process causes the unit's Strength, Dexterity, Attack, Defense, and Ranged

Attack to be reduced by 50 percent. The Zombie unit "dies" at the end of combat.

It goes without saying that this spell is only useful if the dead unit is particularly powerful. Cast this spell on a unit that was mediocre in life, and it becomes even more useless in its undead form.

GENERAL SPELL BOOK

DISPEL MAGIC

Mana Cost: 2

Research Cost: 42

Spell Type: Both

Target: Enchantment

Except for the reduced casting cost, this spell is identical to Air's Dispel Magic.

DETECT LIFE

Mana Cost: 4

Research Cost: 50

Spell Type: World Map

Target: Caster

Detect Life reveals the location of all Life units within a radius of 20 map units of the caster.

PURGE WOUNDS

Mana Cost: 4

Research Cost: 90

Spell Type: World Map

Target: Party

Purge Wounds increases the rate at which a party heals by two Hit Points per turn when the party is not moving. The spell lasts for three turns.

TELEPORT ARTIFACT

Mana Cost: 7

Research Cost: 92

Spell Type: World Map

Target: Caster

Except for its higher mana and research costs, this spell is identical to Air's Teleport Artifact.

OVERLAND SPELL BOOK

FUNERAL MARCH

Mana Cost: 2

Research Cost: 18

Spell Type: World Map

Target: Party

Funeral March increases the target party's movement by 25 percent for the current turn.

Use this spell when your Mages have mana to spare.

RAISE SKELETON

Mana Cost: 6

Research Cost: 26

Spell Type: Combat

Target: Single Dead Unit

The targeted unit is permanently raised as a Skeleton under the caster's control. This is quite a good deal, as it allows you to gain a capable warrior for free. If the battle is won and you have mana to spare, always make use of this spell! Refer to Chapter 7 for details on Skeletons' combat abilities.

SPAWN CAVE

Mana Cost: 6

Research Cost: 30

Spell Type: World Map

Target: Cave

If the target cave has already been conquered, Spawn Cave repopulates the cave with Death creatures. The cave's new strength is equal to the caster's level.

This spell can be useful when you're itching for a fight, but you want to keep your main army close to a Capital. Just cast this spell on a local cave, and you've got yourself some instant conflict!

LOCUST SWARM

Mana Cost: 6

Research Cost: 151

Spell Type: World Map

Target: Party

All units in the targeted party sustain damage points equal to four plus one fifth of the caster's level.

This potent spell is ideal for softening up an army before attacking. By fleeing from the targeted army, you can often get in multiple Locust Swarms before initiating combat.

115

PESTILENCE

Mana Cost: 10

Research Cost: 192

Spell Type: World Map

Target: Party

All units in the targeted party take damage points equal to five plus one half of the caster's level. In addition, the terrain that the targeted party is located on is changed to swamp for a number of turns equal to one plus one half of the caster's level.

This is another great spell for softening up the enemy before moving in for the kill. It's one of the most powerful ways to deal damage to parties on the main map.

RAISE SHADE

Mana Cost: 12

Research Cost: 192

Spell Type: Combat

Target: Single Dead Unit

Raise Shade causes the target dead unit to be raised as a Death Shade under the control of the caster. The Death Shade remains after the combat ends, unless, of course, it is "killed" first.

Death Shades are Death's second-level summoned creature. They're quite effective in combat, so this is a particularly powerful spell. Refer to Chapter 7 for full combat statistics on Death Shades.

If your Mage has enough mana remaining at the end of combat, there's no reason why not to cast this spell after every battle.

EARTH SPELLS

Earth spells are, by and large, very functional. From low-cost spells that enhance units' combat abilities to a number of spells designed to slow, immobilize, or otherwise impair enemy units, Earth's spell repertoire is formidable and practical. Unlike Fire's and Chaos's spells, which bestow large combat bonuses but also confer severe penalties, Earth's spells rarely have major drawbacks.

Fig. 5-4. Here's the Earth spell hierarchy.

ATTACK	DEFENSE	GENERAL	OVERLAND
Rocksling	Stone Hands	Teleport Artifact	Trailblaze
Earthbind	Stone Skin	Poultice	Ranger's Vision
Slow	Create Rocks	Dispel Magic	Detect Cave
Entanglement	Earth Meld	Detect Air	Gold Rush
Sands of Sleep			Clay Earth
Turn to Stone			Earthquake

ATTACK SPELL BOOK

ROCKSLING

Mana Cost: 2

Research Cost: 11

Spell Type: Combat

Target: Single Unit

Rocksling deals damage to the target unit equal to three plus one fourth of the caster's level. This is another direct-damage spell that can be used to pick off weak units or whittle down strong ones. It's one of the less powerful spells of its type.

EARTH BIND

Mana Cost: 2

Research Cost: 14

Spell Type: Combat

Target: Single Air Unit

Earth Bind temporarily slows the Air target unit and deals it three points of damage. This is a highly specific spell, but quite effective when you deal with Air enemies. It combines the punch of Rocksling with the powerful effects of Slow.

SLOW

Mana Cost: 4

Research Cost: 19

Spell Type: Combat

Target: Single Unit

As the name suggests, this spell temporarily slows down enemies in combat.

Aside from the research and casting costs, this spell is identical to Air's spell Headwind. It can be used for the same purposes, such as breaking up groups of enemies or buying your missile troops more time to fire.

ENTANGLEMENT

Mana Cost: 4

Research Cost: 28

Spell Type: Combat

Target: Single Non-Flying Unit

The targeted unit can still attack and cast spells, but cannot move for a limited time.

This is an extreme version of Slow, which forces its target to stick in one place for a given period of time. Anything you can do with Slow, you can do with Entanglement—except that Entanglement doesn't work on flying units. However, this spell is excellent for entrapping escaping units.

SANDS OF SLEEP

Mana Cost: 8
Research Cost: 125
Spell Type: Combat
Target: Area

Sands of Sleep targets a single unit, but all units within the area of effect are temporarily put to sleep. Sleeping units can neither move nor attack. If a sleeping unit is attacked, it wakes up.

Truly a great spell, Sands of Sleep is best used when you cast it into dense enemy clusters. Missile and melee troops are both suitable targets. As with Slow and Entanglement, Sands of Sleep is great for breaking up groups of melee attackers—in this case, by putting some of them to sleep so that they fall behind the rest.

When you put the enemy to sleep, be careful to micromanage your own troops and position all of them before letting any one of them strike the sleeper. Instead of having one attacker strike the enemy, have three or more do the job, and you'll make short work of him, even though he wakes up as a result of the blows. If you have lone units attack sleepers, you'll simply wake them up, and you won't get the most out of this spell.

TURN TO STONE

Mana Cost: 10

Research Cost: 142

Spell Type: Combat

Target: Single Unit

In order for the spell to function at all, the caster must be at least three levels higher than the targeted unit. If this condition is satisfied, the targeted unit is temporarily turned to stone; it can neither move nor attack. This spell is a great way to neutralize a lower-level enemy that poses a threat.

DEFENSE SPELL BOOK

STONE HANDS

Mana Cost: 2

Research Cost: 4

Spell Type: Combat

Target: Single Unit

Stone Hands grants the target unit a temporary +3 bonus to Attack.

This is a basic combat spell that's extremely useful in the game's early stages.

STONE SKIN

Mana Cost: 2

Research Cost: 5

Spell Type: Combat

Target: Single Unit

Stone Skin temporarily adds two points of Defense to the target.

Again, this is a great, simple combat spell that's extremely helpful, especially in the early stages of the game. Cast this and Stone Hands on a unit, and you'll see a marked improvement.

CREATE ROCKS

Mana Cost: 4

Research Cost: 51

Spell Type: Combat

Target: Location

Create Rocks causes rocks to sprout from the ground at the targeted location. Rocks impede movement and block the line of sight.

This spell can be used for a variety of applications. Rocks can force big mobs of enemy melee troops to approach you in a single-file line instead of as a dense mob. They can also present a barrier that delays the enemy while your units escape.

EARTH MELD

Mana Cost: 8

Research Cost: 106

Spell Type: Combat

Target: Single Unit

Earth Meld removes the target unit from combat. Once combat is over, the unit appears as its own group on the overland map.

This is a good spell for saving high-level units that are taking a beating. Experienced troops are infinitely more valuable than low-level troops—the value of this spell should be clear.

GENERAL SPELL BOOK

TELEPORT ARTIFACT

Mana Cost: 2

Research Cost: 21

Spell Type: World Map

Target: Caster

Except for the higher research cost, this spell is identical to Air's Teleport Artifact.

POULTICE

Mana Cost: 4

Research Cost: 26

Spell Type: World Map

Target: Party

Poultice increases the rate at which the target party heals by two Hit Points per turn when the party does not move for the next three turns.

DISPEL MAGIC

Mana Cost: 4

Research Cost: 42

Spell Type: Both

Target: Enchantment

This spell is identical to Air's Dispel Magic.

DETECT AIR

Mana Cost: 4

Research Cost: 50

Spell Type: World Map

Target: Caster

Detect Air reveals the location of all Air units within a radius of 20 map units of the caster.

OVERLAND SPELL BOOK

TRAILBLAZE

Mana Cost: 2

Research Cost: 19

Spell Type: World Map

Target: Party

Trailblaze increases the target party's movement by 25 percent for the current turn.

This spell is very important for the Earth player, as it increases his ability to travel around Urak.

RANGER'S VISION

Mana Cost: 2

Research Cost: 24

Spell Type: World Map

Target: Caster

For the current turn, the caster's sight radius is increased in map units by three plus one third of the caster's level. In addition to the cost of two mana, Ranger's Vision also expends the caster's remaining movement points. You should cast this spell after your Mage's movement points are all but gone, or immediately if your Mage doesn't have to go anywhere that turn.

Mages who travel with armies tend to have more movement points than the sluggish infantry that forms the bulk of the army. Often, your Mage can still cast this spell even after the army has moved as far as it can go on a given turn.

DETECT CAVE

Mana Cost: 4

Research Cost: 33

Spell Type: World Map

Target: None

Detect Cave reveals the closest undiscovered, unseen cave.

This is sometimes a useful spell if you're itching for combat and don't know who to fight.

GOLD RUSH

Mana Cost: 4

Research Cost: 45

Spell Type: World Map

Target: Capital

Gold Rush increases gold production of the targeted Capital by one plus one third of the caster's level.

Gold Rush is the most profitable spell of its type. Most production-enhancing spells only increase resource production by one per turn, but this spell has the potential to increase production by four per turn.

CLAY EARTII

Mana Cost: 8

Research Cost: 112

Spell Type: World Map

Target: Location

Clay Earth turns the target location into mountains, Earth's native terrain.

Terrain-changing spells allow any faith to gain a movement bonus outside of its normal territory.

EARTHQUAKE

Mana Cost: 12

Research Cost: 211

Spell Type: World Map

Target: Party

Earthquake deals damage equal to four plus one fourth of the caster's level to all units in the targeted party.

This is an extremely potent spell for weakening enemy parties before attacking them.

FIRE SPELLS

Fire's combat repertoire includes a number of extremely cheap spells that enhance combat statistics but also cause damage or confer other drawbacks. Spells that damage all units in combat—even those on the caster's side—are common, too. The bottom line is that Fire spells must be cast with a modicum of forethought. If cast recklessly, these spells can cause more harm than good!

Fig. 5-5. This is Fire's spell hierarchy.

ATTACK	DEFENSE	GENERAL	OVERLAND
Fire Dart	Immolation	Cauterize Wounds	Wildfire
Fury Fire	Frenzy	Teleport Artifact	Fireworks
Meat Metal	Flame Sword	Dispel Magic	Lava Flow
Firestorm	Heat Shield	Detect Water	Meteor Shower
Fireball	Burning Skin		
Flame Arrow			
Inferno			

ATTACK SPELL BOOK

FLAME DART

Mana Cost: 2

Research Cost: 5

Spell Type: Combat

Target: Single Unit

Flame Dart deals damage points equal to three plus one third of the caster's level to the targeted unit.

This is a typical direct-damage spell. Use it to kill weak enemies outright or to weaken tough ones.

FURY FIRE

Mana Cost: 4

Research Cost: 100

Spell Type: Combat

Target: Location

Fury Fire causes a fireball to circle the targeted location, dealing two points of damage to everything it hits.

This is an interesting spell because it affects multiple enemies, yet costs less—and deals less damage—than other area-effect damage spells. As always with spells that affect an area, this spell is best cast on a spot packed with enemies. It's particularly good at taking out clusters of missile troops, which are typically fragile.

HEAT METAL

Mana Cost: 4

Research Cost: 36

Spell Type: Combat

Target: Single Unit

Heat Metal deals five points of damage to the target unit. If the target unit is an Earth or Order unit, Heat Metal deals damage relative to the targeted unit's Armor.

Against faiths other than Earth or Order, this spell is average at best. (A high-level Mage would do better to cast a Flame Dart instead.) But against these two faiths, the spell truly shines, especially against heavily armored melee troops. (Note that Armor is a prime component of a unit's Defense rating; this subject is examined more thoroughly in Chapter 7.)

FIRE STORM

Mana Cost: 4

Research Cost: 75

Spell Type: Combat

Target: All Units

Fire Storm deals two points of damage to all units in combat, including your own units.

This spell is ideal when you face a large horde of relatively fragile enemies. And even if your enemies aren't that fragile, this can be a good spell as long as your enemies are numerous and your own troops are healthy.

Do the math before casting this spell. A Level 6 Mage could cast two Flame Darts for four mana and deal a total of 10 damage points between one or two units. On the other hand, that same Mage could cast a single Fire Storm against an enemy of 12 individuals and cause a total of 24 damage points (two to each enemy). The damage from Fire Storm isn't concentrated on one or two units as it would be from a Flame Dart, but the total damage is much higher.

Of course, you also deal considerable damage to your own troops with Fire Storm. That's why small armies of individually tough units are the best casters of this spell.

FIREBALL

Mana Cost: 4
Research Cost: 93
Spell Type: Combat
Target: Single Unit

Fireball deals damage points equal to four plus one half of the caster's level against the target unit.

Think of it as a really big Flame Dart.

FLAME ARROW

Mana Cost: 10
Research Cost: 110
Spell Type: Combat
Target: Area

Flame Arrow targets a single unit, but anything within its radius sustains four points of damage. Of these four points, one point of damage is completely unaffected by any magic resistance the target may have. The spell's radius increases with the caster's level.

As always, aim for big groups when you cast spells like these. Be careful not to shoot a Flame Arrow too close to your own troops!

INFERNO

Mana Cost: 8
Research Cost: 153
Spell Type: Combat
Target: All Units

Inferno causes all units in the battle to sustain twice the caster's level in points of damage.

This spell is good in losing battles where you just want to injure the enemy as much as possible with little regard for your own Mage. A final confrontation with Balkoth would be an ideal scenario for such a spell.

DEFENSE SPELL BOOK

IMMOLATION

Mana Cost: 2
Research Cost: 4
Spell Type: Combat
Target: One Unit

Immolation causes a unit to gain four points of Attack and 25 percent missile resistance. However, the unit suffers a loss of two Defense points as well.

FRENZY

Mana Cost: 2

Research Cost: 7

Spell Type: Combat

Target: Single Unit

The target of Frenzy permanently loses three Hit Points and also sustains a random number of damage points (up to four plus one third of the caster's level). The target unit then temporarily gains Attack points equal to three plus a random number between zero and one half of the caster's level. The unit also gains Ranged Attack equal to one plus a random number between zero and one half of the caster's level and Defense equal to two plus a random number between zero and one half of the caster's level.

FLAME SWORD

Mana Cost: 2

Research Cost: 10

Spell Type: Combat

Target: Single Unit

Flame Sword grants the target unit a +3 bonus to Attack.

This spell is a much safer way to increase your units' combat ability than Frenzy and Immolation are.

HEAT SHIELD

Mana Cost: 4

Research Cost: 43

Spell Type: Combat

Target: Single Unit

Heat Shield adds two points to the target unit's Defense and grants the target a 50 percent or greater missile resistance.

Be sure that your army faces at least a few missile troops before casting this spell because the relatively high casting cost can't justify the Defense bonus alone.

BURNING SKIN

Mana Cost: 8

Research Cost: 36

Spell Type: Combat

Target: Caster

For a short while, Burning Skin causes any unit striking the caster to sustain in damage points a number equal to one half of the caster's level.

This is a great spell to cast on a tough, well-armored melee unit that plunges into the forefront of battle. It's important that this unit be tough enough to take some abuse because, if it's killed with just one or two hits, you won't get much value from the spell.

GENERAL SPELL BOOK

CAUTERIZE WOUNDS

Mana Cost: 2

Research Cost: 20

Spell Type: World Map

Target: Party

Cauterize Wounds increases the rate at which the party heals by two Hit Points when the party is not moving over the next three turns.

TELEPORT ARTIFACT

Mana Cost: 4

Research Cost: 22

Spell Type: World Map

Target: Caster

Aside from the higher casting and research costs, this spell is identical to Air's Teleport Artifact.

DISPEL MAGIC

Mana Cost: 4

Research Cost: 42

Spell Type: Both

Target: Enchantment

This spell is identical to Air's Dispel Magic.

DETECT WATER

Mana Cost: 4

Research Cost: 50

Spell Type: World Map

Target: Caster

Detect Water reveals the locations of all Water units within a radius of 20 map units of the caster.

OVERLAND SPELL BOOK

WILDFIRE

Mana Cost: 2

Research Cost: 26

Spell Type: World Map

Target: Party

Wildfire increases the target party's movement by 25 percent for the current turn.

As usual, cast this spell near the beginning of a turn in which your Mages aren't likely to need their mana points for combat.

FIREWORKS

Mana Cost: 4

Research Cost: 45

Spell Type: World Map

Target: Capital

Fireworks increases the fame production of the targeted Capital by one point.

Cast this spell regularly when your Mages have little else to do.

LAVA FLOW

Mana Cost: 6

Research Cost: 64

Spell Type: World Map

Target: Location

Lava Flow turns the target location into lava, Fire's native terrain.

Use this spell to convert terrain to Fire-friendly lava and to gain movement bonuses for your Fire troops.

METEOR SHOWER

Mana Cost: 10

Research Cost: 133

Spell Type: World Map

Target: Party

Meteor Shower deals in damage points a number equal to three plus one half of the caster's level to all units in the targeted party.

This spell is typically used for damaging enemy parties before attacking them.

LIFE SPELLS

Life's unique spells tend to emphasize healing. While healing is admittedly not as exciting as flashy Attack spells, it's a very efficient way of enhancing your battlefield prowess. It allows powerful combat units to survive longer and strike more frequently—a single blow from a good melee attacker is often equal to the damage a costly attack spell would cause.

Furthermore, healing spells—not to mention the potent Resurrection—help preserve experienced troops. These troops rank among the game's most valuable commodities; anything you can do to preserve them is a step in the right direction.

Fig. 5-6. Here's the Life spell hierarchy.

ATTACK	DEFENSE	GENERAL	OVERLAND
Spirit Arrow	Protect	Purify Wounds	Commune With Nature
Bless	Cure Wounds	Teleport Artifact	Holy Enchantment
Turn Undead	Blessing	Dispel Magic	Sanctuary
Ray of Hope	Heal	Detect Death	Invigorate
	Regeneration	Resurrection	Create Plains
	Holy Visit		

ATTACK SPELL BOOK

SPIRIT ARROW

Mana Cost: 2

Research Cost: 5

Spell Type: Combat

Target: Single Unit

Spirit Arrow deals three plus one half of the caster's level in points of damage to the target unit.

This ranks among the more potent low-level, direct-damage spells available.

BLESS

Mana Cost: 4

Research Cost: 22

Spell Type: Combat

Target: All Units

Bless temporarily grants all Life units +2 to Attack and +1 to Defense while forcing Death units to fight at −2 Attack.

Thanks to the low casting cost, Bless is useful even when you are not fighting the legions of Death. When you fight Death units, however, this spell is particularly potent. Just bear in mind that if your army consists of both Life units and units from another faith, the latter units won't enjoy the benefits of Bless.

TURN UNDEAD

Mana Cost: 4

Research Cost: 115

Spell Type: Combat

Target: Single Undead Unit

Turn Undead deals three times the caster's level in points of damage to all undead units in combat (up to a maximum of nine points).

Though specialized, this spell is—hands down—the most efficient way of dealing with Skeletons, Death Shades, and Vampires.

RAY OF HOPE

Mana Cost: 8

Research Cost: 192

Spell Type: Combat

Target: Area

Ray of Hope targets a single unit, but anything within its radius sustains damage equal to four plus one fourth of the caster's level. The spell's radius increases with the caster's level.

This is a good area-effect spell for damaging dense crowds of enemies. As always, be careful not to cast it too close to your own units!

DEFENSE SPELL BOOK

PROTECT

Mana Cost: 2
Research Cost: 16
Spell Type: Combat
Target: Single Unit

Protect grants the target unit a +50 bonus to missile resistance.

This is a good spell to cast on any units attacking missile troops or on your faith's Lord (if he happens to be in combat).

CURE WOUNDS

Mana Cost: 2
Research Cost: 17
Spell Type: Both
Target: Single Unit

Cure Wounds heals three plus one third of the caster's level in points of damage. This spell has no effect on undead units.

Healing spells aren't as exciting as attack spells, but they can often be much more potent. If your army features tough, high-level melee attackers or missile troops, healing these troops—and thus allowing them to continue attacking the enemy—usually results in much more damage to the enemy than blasting them with offensive spells.

BLESSING

Mana Cost: 4

Research Cost: 25

Spell Type: Combat

Target: Single Unit

Blessing grants a temporary Defense bonus of three plus one third of the caster's level.

This is a potent spell capable of making a fragile unit tough, or a tough unit even tougher. It's particularly effective in the game's early stages, where even a small bonus is of great value.

HEAL

Mana Cost: 4

Research Cost: 121

Spell Type: Both

Target: Single Unit

Heal cures the target anywhere from one to four times the caster's level in points of damage. Heal has no affect on undead units.

Whereas Cure Wounds can heal up to seven Hit Points of damage (when cast by a twelfth-level Lord), Heal can cure up to 48 points (when cast by the same Lord and the spell happens to work perfectly). Since Heal costs twice as much as Cure Wounds and involves an element of chance, Cure Wounds is usually preferable when the target only requires moderate healing.

REGENERATION

Mana Cost: 8
Research Cost: 129
Spell Type: Combat
Target: Single Unit

Regeneration heals the target unit of one point of damage every three seconds for up to one minute (for a maximum of 20 points of healing). This spell will not bring a dead unit back to life.

This is a good spell to cast on a front-line unit that receives considerable punishment. If that unit is already severely damaged, however, and needs instant healing, Heal may be a better choice of spells.

You can also cast this spell near the end of combat when there's only token resistance left. This more thoroughly heals damaged units before proceeding to the next battle.

HOLY VISIT

Mana Cost: 8
Research Cost: 160
Spell Type: Combat
Target: All Units

Holy Visit heals all friendly units of four plus one half of the caster's level in points of damage. It also causes all enemy units to fight temporarily with a –2 Attack penalty. (The –2 penalty sticks with Death permanently.)

This is truly a great spell to cast in the middle of combat, when your front line of melee troops is busy fighting the enemy's front line. It's at this time—before you have sustained serious casualties, but after your troops have been seriously wounded—that this spell is most effective.

General Spell Book

Purify Wounds

Mana Cost: 2

Research Cost: 18

Spell Type: World Map

Target: Party

Purify Wounds increases the rate at which the party heals by three Hit Points when the party is not moving for the next three turns.

Teleport Artifact

Mana Cost: 4

Research Cost: 30

Spell Type: World Map

Target: Caster

Except for the higher casting and research costs, this spell is identical to Air's Teleport Artifact.

Dispel Magic

Mana Cost: 4

Research Cost: 42

Spell Type: Both

Target: Enchantment

This spell is identical to Air's Dispel Magic.

DETECT DEATH

Mana Cost: 8

Research Cost: 50

Spell Type: World Map

Target: Caster

Detect Death reveals the location of all Death units within a radius of 20 map units of the caster.

RESURRECTION

Mana Cost: 12

Research Cost: 192

Spell Type: Combat

Target: Single Dead Unit in your army

The target unit is brought back to life with four plus one half of the caster's level in Hit Points. Resurrection does not work on undead units.

Since high-level, experienced troops are invaluable in Lords of Magic, any spells that allow you to restore them to "life" is powerful indeed. Resurrection is no exception.

OVERLAND SPELL BOOK

COMMUNE WITH NATURE

Mana Cost: 2

Research Cost: 12

Spell Type: World Map

Target: Caster

In addition to the two mana, Commune With Nature also expends the caster's remaining movement points. For the current turn, the caster's sight radius is increased by three plus one third of his level in map units.

141

Use this spell only after your Mage has moved or when he doesn't have to move. Mages who travel with armies usually have more movement points than the slowest members of the army and, thus, will still have movement points to burn after the army has finished moving.

HOLY ENCHANTMENT

Mana Cost: 2

Research Cost: 22

Spell Type: World Map

Target: Capital

Holy Enchantment increases the fame output of the targeted Capital by one plus one third of the caster's level.

As always, cast this type of spell whenever your Mages have mana to spare.

SANCTUARY

Mana Cost: 4

Research Cost: 30

Spell Type: World Map

Target: Capital

Sanctuary increases the sight radius of the targeted Capital by one plus one third of the caster's level to a maximum total of seven.

This is a good spell for times when you aren't sure whether an attack is imminent and when you don't have the available manpower to scout around your Capital.

INVIGORATE

Mana Cost: 4

Research Cost: 39

Spell Type: World Map

Target: Party

Invigorate increases the target party's movement by 25 percent for the current turn.

Always cast movement-enhancing spells before the target unit starts to move for that turn.

CREATE PLAIN

Mana Cost: 8

Research Cost: 135

Spell Type: World Map

Target: Location

Create Plain turns the target location into meadows, Life's native terrain.

Cast this spell to create terrain that's easy for your Life units to cross.

ORDER SPELLS

Order features a number of potent and functional combat spells that increase friendly units' combat stats and summon potent creatures. Unusual spells, such as Possession and Heroic Demise, further increase the potency of Order's combat-spell lineup.

All things considered, Order spells rank among the best and most focused spells in combat.

Fig. 5-7. This chart shows the Order spell hierarchy.

ATTACK	DEFENSE	GENERAL	OVERLAND
Righteous Bolt	Leadership	First Aid	Falcon's Eye
Righteous Cause	Protection	Teleport Artifact	Forced March
Justice	Reflection Shield	Dispel Magic	Inspire
Summon Spirit Warrior	Heroic Demise	Detect Chaos	Watch Tower
Possession	Crusade	Seer	Survey

ATTACK SPELL BOOK

RIGHTEOUS BOLT

Mana Cost: 2

Research Cost: 5

Spell Type: Combat

Target: Single Unit

Righteous Bolt deals damage points equal to three plus one third of the caster's level to a single target.

This is a standard direct-damage spell.

RIGHTEOUS CAUSE

Mana Cost: 4

Research Cost: 14

Spell Type: Combat

Target: Single Unit

Righteous Cause temporarily grants the target unit +4 to Attack and +2 to Ranged Attack. It also adds +1 to Defense.

This is a well-balanced spell best used when it's cast on melee troops. Use it to gain the upper hand in close, hard-fought battles.

JUSTICE

Mana Cost: 4

Research Cost: 57

Spell Type: Combat

Target: Area

Justice targets a single unit, but anything caught within its radius sustains damage points equal to three plus one third of the caster's level. The spell's radius varies according to the caster's level.

As is always the case with area-effect spells, cast this one into dense crowds, or stick with Righteous Bolt.

SUMMON SPIRIT WARRIOR

Mana Cost: 8

Research Cost: 124

Spell Type: Combat

Target: None

Summon Spirit Warrior summons a Warrior Spirit that fights on the side of the caster for the duration of combat.

Warrior Spirits are the most powerful summoned units available to Order; they're capable of turning the tide of battle in a real hurry! Unlike Death spells that summon creatures, this spell doesn't keep the creature around after combat has ended. That's a shame, but on the other hand, this spell gives you a much more powerful creature than Death's spells can offer.

Cast this spell like crazy—it's a great value!

POSSESSION

Mana Cost: 10

Research Cost: 165

Spell Type: Combat

Target: Single Unit

Possession causes the target unit, which must be at least two levels lower than the caster, to come under the caster's control. The possessed unit dies at the end of combat even if it is the last unit left in combat.

Like Summon Spirit Warrior, this spell is a hands-down winner. The ability to take control of an enemy unit (preferably the most powerful one you can get your hands on) can't be argued with. Possessed units must be at a lower level than the caster, it's true—but if you have a twelfth-level Mage Lord on your side, just about anything short of another Lord can come under this spell's influence.

DEFENSE SPELL BOOK

LEADERSHIP

Mana Cost: 2

Research Cost: 14

Spell Type: Combat

Target: All Friendly Units

Leadership temporarily increases the Attack of all friendly units by one.

This is a great spell for the cost if you have a big army. In small armies, its value is less apparent.

PROTECTION

Mana Cost: 2

Research Cost: 16

Spell Type: Combat

Target: All Friendly Units

Protection temporarily increases the Defense of all friendly units by one.

Like Leadership, this spell is a great value for medium to large armies. Cast both spells at the beginning of combat to fortify your army.

REFLECTION SHIELD

Mana Cost: 4

Research Cost: 86

Spell Type: Combat

Target: Single Unit

Reflection Shield temporarily grants the target unit +50 percent missile resistance.

Cast this spell on valuable units or front runners trying to attack enemy missile troops. It's fairly expensive and has a very specialized application. Don't cast it unless the enemy has a legitimate number of missile troops under his command.

HEROIC DEMISE

Mana Cost: 8
Research Cost: 122
Spell Type: Combat
Target: Single Unit

Heroic Demise adds six to both the Attack and Defense of the target unit. Unfortunately, the target unit dies at the end of combat.

This spell was made for mercenaries. By hiring mercenaries and then casting this spell on 'em, you end up with do-it-yourself super troops. Of course, the "beneficiary" of this spell dies at the end of combat—but since it's just a lowly mercenary, who cares! In some cases, killing off your mercenaries is even desirable; this spell just adds an extra incentive.

CRUSADE

Mana Cost: 10
Research Cost: 151
Spell Type: Combat
Target: All Units

Crusade temporarily adds four to the Attack, Missile Attack, and Defense of all friendly units.

This is a very potent spell. Cast it at the beginning of combat for maximum effect.

GENERAL SPELL BOOK

FIRST AID

Mana Cost: 2

Research Cost: 16

Spell Type: World Map

Target: Party

First Aid increases the rate at which the target party heals by two Hit Points when the party's not moving for the next three turns.

TELEPORT ARTIFACT

Mana Cost: 2

Research Cost: 20

Spell Type: World Map

Target: Caster

Except for the higher research cost, this spell is identical to Air's Teleport Artifact.

DISPEL MAGIC

Mana Cost: 4

Research Cost: 42

Spell Type: Both

Target: Enchantment

This spell is identical to Air's Dispel Magic.

DETECT CHAOS

Mana Cost: 4

Research Cost: 50

Spell Type: World Map

Target: Caster

Detect Chaos reveals the location of all Chaos units within a radius of 20 map units of the caster.

SEER

Mana Cost: 4

Research Cost: 75

Spell Type: World Map

Target: Location

Seer reveals the terrain and the presence of any Death, Fire, or Earth units in a radius of 10 map units of the targeted location.

OVERLAND SPELL BOOK

FALCON'S EYE

Mana Cost: 2

Research Cost: 15

Spell Type: World Map

Target: Caster

In addition to the two mana, Falcon's Eye also expends the caster's remaining movement points. For the current turn, the caster's sight radius is increased in map units by three plus one third of the caster's level.

As usual with spells that require movement points and mana, cast this spell after burning most of your Mage's movement points for the turn.

FORCED MARCH

Mana Cost: 2

Research Cost: 18

Spell Type: World Map

Target: Party

Forced March increases the target party's movement by 25 percent for the current turn.

This is a typical movement-enhancing spell that should be cast at the beginning of a turn when your Mages have spare mana and you probably won't need it in combat.

INSPIRE

Mana Cost: 4

Research Cost: 45

Spell Type: World Map

Target: Capital

Inspire increases the production of ale, crystals, and gold in the target Capital by one each turn for the next three turns.

This is, hands down, the most powerful production-enhancing spell available, as it enhances production of all three resources simultaneously.

WATCH TOWER

Mana Cost: 4

Research Cost: 42

Spell Type: World Map

Target: Capital

Watch Tower increases the targeted Capital's sight radius by one plus one third of the caster's level in map units. The Capital's sight radius cannot be increased by more than seven map units.

SURVEY

Mana Cost: 8

Research Cost: 135

Spell Type: World Map

Target: Location

Survey turns the target location into plains, Order's native terrain.

Plains enhance Order units' movement while slowing down Chaos and Earth units.

WATER SPELLS

Water has a number of useful healing spells. It also has spells that confer a benefit to one unit while damaging another unit, and spells that provide benefits but also have certain drawbacks. Water's spells can be used in combinations very neatly. In fact, successful use of certain spells almost depends on using them in conjunction with other spells.

Fig. 5-8. This is the hierarchy for Water spells

ATTACK	DEFENSE	GENERAL	OVERLAND
Ice Bolt	Light Rain	Teleport Artifact	Riptide
Blood Lust	Quick Silver	Cleanse Wounds	Whisper of the Waves
Rust	Heal Self	Dispel Magic	Fog
Freeze	Steam Cloud	Detect Fire	Create Land
	Gift of Life	Seer	Healing Waters
	Guardian Waves		

ATTACK SPELL BOOK

ICE BOLT

Mana Cost: 2

Research Cost: 5

Spell Type: Combat

Target: Single Unit

Ice Bolt deals three plus one third of the caster's level in damage points against a single target.

This is a typical direct-damage spell.

BLOOD LUST

Mana Cost: 4

Research Cost: 27

Spell Type: Combat

Target: Single Unit

Blood Lust greatly increases the target unit's Attack and Defense, but the actual amount varies. This spell's drawback is that the unit also takes one point of damage for every two seconds in combat.

This is a great spell to cast on mercenaries, as mercenaries are completely expendable.

RUST

Mana Cost: 4

Research Cost: 81

Spell Type: Combat

Target: Single Unit

Rust reduces the target unit's Defense value by three points.

Melee troops are the logical targets for this spell. Missile troops and Mages are fragile to begin with and can be torn apart easily by mediocre melee troops. It's the tough, well-armored melee troops that need to be brought down a notch, and this is the spell to do it.

FREEZE

Mana Cost: 10

Research Cost: 120

Spell Type: Combat

Target: Single Unit

Freeze encases the targeted unit in ice. This has two major effects: first, the target cannot move or attack; second, the target becomes immune to missile and melee attacks (but not to spell attacks). Based on the caster's level, this spell's duration varies.

The fact that missile and melee attacks won't affect a frozen unit may make this spell sound unappealing, but consider that you can target any unit, regardless of level differences, with Freeze. Thus, you could Freeze an enemy Lord and deal with his army before turning your undivided attention to him. Or, you could pelt the aforementioned Lord with damaging spells while he's frozen.

The key to making this spell count is to target the enemy that's far and away the most powerful. Groups of homogenous enemies won't be affected too much by Freeze. Note that this spell can also be used to protect your own damaged units.

Defense Spell Book

Light Rain

Mana Cost: 2

Research Cost: 14

Spell Type: Combat

Target: Single Fire Unit

Light Rain temporarily slows the target Fire unit and deals it three points of damage.

This is a very inexpensive way of dealing two adverse effects to an enemy. The hitch, of course, is that this spell works on Fire units only. But if and when you encounter a Fire unit, this ranks among the best spells to attack it with.

Quick Silver

Mana Cost: 2

Research Cost: 16

Spell Type: Combat

Target: Single Unit

Quick Silver temporarily increases the target unit's speed when it moves across adverse terrain. The caster's level determines this spell's duration.

Cast this spell on units about to traverse hilly or otherwise difficult terrain. Combine this spell with Riptide to make a unit extremely mobile.

HEAL SELF

Mana Cost: 4

Research Cost: 48

Spell Type: Both

Target: Caster

If the caster is at more than 50 percent health, Heal Self restores the caster to full health; otherwise, the caster gains 50 percent of his maximum Hit Points.

This spell is a great way of keeping your spellcaster alive. If enemy melee troops catch up with your spellcaster, he probably will be cut down regardless of how many times you heal him. This spell, however, is good for repairing incidental damage from missiles and enemy spells.

STEAM CLOUD

Mana Cost: 4

Research Cost: 61

Spell Type: Combat

Target: Caster

Steam Cloud creates a temporary cloud of steam around the caster that deals three damage points to any unit that strikes the caster.

This is a fairly risky spell, as it requires you to put your spellcaster in danger and, in fact, to take some abuse in order to hurt others. When it's cast in conjunction with Guardian Waves (which helps defend the caster) and Heal Self (which repairs damage to the caster), the caster becomes a veritable wrecking machine.

GIFT OF LIFE

Mana Cost: 2

Research Cost: 83

Spell Type: Combat

Target: Single Unit

Gift of Life deals four damage points to the caster and heals the target unit's damage points in an amount equal to four plus one third of the caster's level.

Cast this spell a few times to heal damaged units and then use Heal Self to restore your Mage to good health. The end result is a much healthier army.

GUARDIAN WAVES

Mana Cost: 8

Research Cost: 129

Spell Type: Combat

Target: Caster

Guardian Waves bestow 50 percent resistance to missile attacks and increases the caster's Defense by two.

This is a fairly good defensive spell, but it's also quite expensive. Cast it on front-line troops that would otherwise be massacred by enemy missile troops.

GENERAL SPELL BOOK

TELEPORT ARTIFACT

Mana Cost: 2

Research Cost: 21

Spell Type: World Map

Target: Caster

Except for the increased research cost, this spell is identical to Air's Teleport Artifact.

CLEANSE WOUNDS

Mana Cost: 2

Research Cost: 36

Spell Type: World Map

Target: Party

Cleanse Wounds increases the rate at which the party heals by three Hit Points when it's not moving over the next three turns.

DISPEL MAGIC

Mana Cost: 4

Research Cost: 42

Spell Type: Both

Target: Enchantment

This spell is identical to Air's Dispel Magic.

DETECT FIRE

Mana Cost: 4

Research Cost: 63

Spell Type: World Map

Target: Caster

All Fire units' locations are revealed within a radius of 15 map units of the caster.

SEER

Mana Cost: 4

Research Cost: 75

Spell Type: World Map

Target: Location

Seer reveals both the terrain and the presence of any Chaos, Death, or Earth units within a radius of 10 map units from the targeted location.

Between Chaos, Earth, and Death units, this spell is capable of revealing most of Water's traditional enemies (with the major exception of Fire).

OVERLAND SPELL BOOK

RIPTIDE

Mana Cost: 2

Research Cost: 22

Spell Type: World Map

Target: Party

Riptide increases the target party's movement by 25 percent for the current turn.

Cast this spell on units before they move, but be sure that your Mages don't need their mana for something else first.

WHISPER OF THE WAVES

Mana Cost: 4

Research Cost: 36

Spell Type: World Map

Target: Location

All Water units are revealed within a radius of 10 map units from the location.

FOG

Mana Cost: 4

Research Cost: 50

Spell Type: World Map

Target: Party

Fog reduces the targeted party's movement and sight radius by two for the current turn.

This spell is a bit more valuable in multiplayer games than in single-player ones, as the reduced sight radius can be devastating to human players.

MAKE LAND

Mana Cost: 8

Research Cost: 58

Spell Type: World Map

Target: Water Location

Make Land turns the target water location into land.

This spell can be useful for creating land bridges that your non-seafaring units can traverse.

HEALING WATERS

Mana Cost: 10
Research Cost: 192
Spell Type: World Map
Target: Party

Healing Waters restores all units in the party to full health. This spell has no effect on undead units.

This is a great, no-nonsense way of healing parties between battles. Its main advantage is its speed—no waiting is necessary.

CHAPTER

EMPIRE BUILDING

his chapter is a grab bag of tips and tricks that will help you build a **Lords of Magic** empire. Every game is different, so we can't present a single formula that holds true for every game. We can, however, give you suggestions on how to build a solid power base that will carry you through the game—and, hopefully, all the way to victory.

Aside from tips on maximizing efficiency in the early, middle, and late stages of the game, this chapter also contains detailed unit comparisons and strategies for beating Balkoth. The unit comparisons will help you build more efficient armies, and the Balkoth strategies will come in handy during the last few turns of your game.

Read Chapter 2 before delving into this chapter. It provides you with a basic outline of how a typical **Lords of Magic** game flows and serves as the foundation for the additional information in this chapter.

INITIAL TROUBLES: TIPS FOR THE EARLY GAME

The game's early stages are usually the hardest. They're difficult because one lost battle or one bad decision could end everything, forcing you to restart. Once you have taken over your Great Temple, your options multiply and the game becomes easier—not necessarily easy, but easier.

Chapter 2 explains a typical strategy for handling the game's early stages, including multiple attacks on low-level caves, hiring mercenaries, and gaining experience until a raid on the Great Temple is feasible. Here are some extra tips to explain this process further.

EARLY TRADES

The Market in your Capital has horrendous exchange rates; in general, trading one resource for another is a bad deal. In games played at the Hard-difficulty setting, you often need specific resources to hire mercenaries; in many cases, however, those resources aren't forthcoming.

What can you do? In some cases, you can travel to a nearby friendly faith and try to barter for the resources you need. This is not a common strategy, but it can be effective.

Trade away your leader's initial artifact or your spells if you're desperate; they are the most valuable things you have. In general, artifacts rank among the best items to trade. During the course of the game, you'll acquire many artifacts, only a few of which can be used at any given time. Trade away those artifacts for valuable resources, as shown in figure 6-1.

If you don't plan to travel great distances for trading purposes, you can still do some trading at your Capital. Sometimes you need just one or two more gold or ale to support a mercenary for one more day—and that day is all-important. In cases where you need only a small amount of a particular resource, your Capital's Market is a good place to trade. In these cases, you can overlook the Market's poor exchange rates because you aren't trading in volume. Just don't make trading at the Market a habit; you'll always get bad deals there.

Fig. 6-1. This Lord has so many artifacts that he's like a walking pawn shop. He needs to trade away some of the less useful items.

LINEAR COMBAT PROGRESSION

It's been stated in Chapter 2, but it should be stated once again: only attack Level 1 caves and mines at the game's beginning. They are infinitely easier to clean out than Level 2 caves, and there is much less of a risk of losing units inside.

Only move up to Level 2 caves after you have completely scoured the area and have attacked all possible Level 1 caves.

DO THE MERCENARY MATH

You can't afford to hire mercenaries indiscriminately in the game's early stages because, every time you hire a mercenary, you assure yourself of a constant resource loss. Once these resources run out, you lose your mercenaries.

Before hiring a mercenary, do the math. Mentally subtract the mercenary's hiring fee from your total resources, and calculate how many turns you'll be able to pay him with your current level of resources. You need at least enough resources to pay your mercenaries until you reach the next combat spot, where you hopefully will earn enough to pay them for a few more turns. Ideally, you should also have a few turns worth of extra resources, so that, if the first combat doesn't yield much loot, you can quickly proceed to a new location.

> Hire as few mercenaries as possible. Ideally, you should hire just enough mercenaries to win each battle without losing your loyal troops.

If your mercenaries devour all your resources, it may seem as though you're getting nowhere (even if you keep traveling from cave to cave and defeating everything that lies within). In fact, you are making progress just as long as you manage to preserve most of your army. That's because the army gains experience as it fights, and experience is crucial when you try to recapture your Great Temple.

PROGRESS-AND-SAVE

Save the game after every small victory in a cave, especially if it yields a fair amount of loot. Incremental game saves are key to getting past the game's brutal early turns on Hard difficulty, and they are quite useful on a game at Medium as well. At the Easy difficulty level, on the other hand, you should be able to blast through several Level 1 caves and retake your Great Temple with minimal game-saves.

TEST THE TEMPLE

Periodically try to attack the Great Temple after saving the game. Do this even when success seems unlikely. The sooner you get the Great Temple, the sooner you can start to accumulate wealth. You don't have to walk on pins and needles once you have taken control of your Great Temple.

MID-GAME TIPS

The middle stages of a typical game are much less rigorous than the ones of the early game. You can usually recover from failed combat attempts and financial troubles during the mid-game stages, thanks to your industrious followers working in your Capital. These followers generate the resources necessary to train new armies and to get back on track.

If you fail during the game's middle stages, it usually won't be immediately obvious. It only becomes apparent later in the game when a huge army—much bigger and better than anything you can muster—shows up at your doorstep. If this happens, you will know that you weren't efficient enough during the mid-game stages and that you probably will have to start the game over.

CRUSH AN ENEMY, CONQUER A FRIEND

When you take over the Great Temple of an ally at the Medium- and Hard-difficulty levels, only a small percentage of that faith's followers will swear allegiance to you; the rest are lost. The net result is fewer troops on your side of the conflict. For example, if you're playing Life and you assimilate Water (another "good" faith), you actually reduce the total number of "good" troops in Urak.

Why take over allies, then? For one thing, having several Capitals under one player's control tends to make things easier. Two faiths that serve under one player never have to worry about coordination—that is, "What's the other faith doing?"—because one leader controls everything on one side, resulting in a more coherent battle plan.

The other main benefit of taking over friendly faiths is that, quite frankly, you're more skillful than the computer-controlled Lords in Urak. You're smarter than they are, and if you have played the game much at all, you're likely to make better strategic decisions than they would make. So, the more faiths under your control, the better.

The bottom line is that you should take over one or two friendly faiths to expand your power base, but you should always try to take over at least one enemy faith for every two friendly faiths under your control. If you go around collecting friendly faiths without attacking enemies, you run the risk of temporarily reducing the total number of "good guys" in Urak; enemy faiths that haven't been similarly depleted can then overwhelm you. Feel free to take over friendly Great Temples—it's an easy way to expand your power base—but try to take over enemy faiths, too.

GUARDING IMPORTANT STRUCTURES

Villages usually aren't worth guarding. The main exception is a Village with a high-level military structure that you have upgraded with considerable resources. These Villages deserve a modicum of defense. A lone scout posted at such a Village can quickly hire mercenaries to respond to any crisis.

Capitals and outlying structures can be defended in much the same way.

DEFENDING CAPITALS

You should never break up your main army to spread units around for defense. Instead, keep your main army in the general vicinity of your Capitals, and have it respond to any emergencies in your territory. Meanwhile, a few defenders should hang around in the vicinity of your Capitals and should hire mercenaries to help respond to any major crises. Mercenaries can completely handle small crises on their own, whereas they'll only serve as a speed bump when handling larger problems. Even when they can't handle it all by themselves, they serve their purpose by slowing down the biggest threats. Larger problems usually require intervention of your main army.

This strategy seemingly leaves your Capitals with little defense, but it works well if you accomplish the following things first:

1. Upgrade and bestow experience upon the Barracks and Thieves' Guilds near your Capitals. When stocked with experience, these structures can produce mid-level mercenaries instantaneously.

2. Try to maintain a good reserve of resources at all times, so that you can hire vast legions of mercenaries at a moment's notice.

3. Have one or two scouts patrol the area around each Capital, so that you can see, and prepare for, approaching armies in time. (See figure 6-2.)

If a Capital is lost despite these precautions, don't worry. Just send down your main army to destroy the invaders and reclaim the Capital. A lost Capital means lost worker production,

Fig. 6-2. A few scouts in the vicinity of your Capital can help detect enemy attacks in advance.

but by retaking the Capital, you can get right back in stride. Losing a Capital for a few turns causes no permanent damage.

DEFENDING OUTLYING STRUCTURES

Renegades like to occupy outlying structures. Have the local Capital's defense force attack Renegades the instant they enter an outlying structure to prevent damage to the structure.

Do note that, unless you have experience stored in a structure, or the structure has been upgraded past Level 1, losing a structure is not a cataclysmic event. Simply retake the demolished structure and pay a nominal fee to restore it to Level 1—and you're back in business!

FRIENDLY NEGOTIATIONS

Try to sell artifacts for extra resources whenever possible. As the game wears on, you probably will find yourself with a veritable pawnshop of artifacts, some useful and some not. Trade the useless artifacts for valuable resources or troops whenever possible.

Also, try to offer gifts to enemies that aren't completely hostile. Refer to the attitude list in Chapter 3 to see the spectrum of possible attitudes. Note the attitude of the faith you're dealing with, and you should get a fairly good sense as to whether an enemy faith can ever be swayed to your side. For example, a faith with a Loathing attitude is usually beyond hope, but Aversion can sometimes be improved upon.

> **Improving relations is a sure-fire ticket to an easy game because you'll have one less enemy to worry about.**

Friendly relations are always worthwhile even if you plan to take over a particular faith in the immediate future. At the very least, good relations will keep you from worrying about attacks from that faith before you decide whether to break the treaty and crush 'em.

TRIMMING THE FAT

As the middle stages of the game continue, you should clean the last vestiges of mercenary troops from your permanent armies. It's still fine to hire the occasional mercenaries for defense in a particularly tough combat, but these mercenaries should not be retained for more than a few turns at a time. They drain your resources too much to be of any long-term value!

The main exception to this rule is when you're in a really tough jam, and enemies are running wild through your territory. In this case, you need combat assistance any way you can get it, and you should retain experienced mercenaries until the crisis is over.

> **Always remember to have mercenaries killed (in battle) instead of dismissing them. That way, you get your full value from them.**

SCOUTING THE LAND

Training scout units doesn't require any loyal followers. In effect, scouts are very cheap, at least compared to standard combat units, which require loyal followers to train. There's no excuse for a lack of scouts! Buy several of them and scour the globe.

FAME: MONEY IN THE BANK

As you continue to expand your empire, remember that your increasing fame is like a piggy bank that, when broken, eventually yields instant gold. You can always sell fame away at the Magistrate's and receive donations in return.

You shouldn't constantly deplete your fame, but sometimes it's essential. The best time to deplete your fame is when your Capitals are full of working followers and, as a result, cannot support any more. In this case, if you can't upgrade your Strongholds with your available gold supply, you should sell enough fame to acquire gold for an upgrade. Your weekly influx of new followers suffer from this loss of fame, but your full-to-the-brim Strongholds could not have gotten much use of these new followers anyway—the loss of fame is minimal.

Selling fame is also a good way to generate revenue for emergency mercenary purchases.

LATE-GAME TIPS

The later stages of the game offer the most opportunity for creativity and personal strategies. By this point, you should have one or two large armies, a few Capitals under your control, and any number of scouts and small parties throughout your lands.

This is the stage of the game where full-scale attacks from enemy faiths—most notably, Balkoth and company—tend to arrive. These massive attacks determine the game's outcome and serve as a litmus test for how well you prepared in the game's earlier stages. If you got off to a slow start or mismanaged your empire during the early and middle stages, you'll pay for it now. On the other hand, if you did a good job, you should be able to stave off Balkoth and his evil compatriots.

> Massive attacks against your Capital tend to come earlier in multiplayer games than in single-player games. Be prepared!

SKILLFUL FOLLOWER ALLOCATION

Allocate your followers in the most productive manner possible; namely, have your followers do the following:

- Have followers produce gold and ale first and foremost, followed by crystal and fame. You need gold and ale to hire mercenaries and to train troops. You also need crystals for these functions, especially if you want to summon creatures.

- Upgrade Strongholds immediately if you no longer have room to put followers to work. Sell fame if necessary!

- Even if you eventually convert your followers into combat units, assign them to work right up until the moment when they're needed at the Barracks.

UPGRADING THE MAIN ARMY

Since your veteran troops are your biggest asset, you can't afford to spread them around, making them vulnerable. Instead, you must keep them together in a single deadly force that can beat just about anything that comes its way.

Feel free to create additional armies if you can support them, but always keep upgrading the main army whenever possible. This requires that you pick winnable fight after winnable fight, building on experience totals without losing any of your army's key members.

After the army's members have collectively achieved a high level, you should look for ways to make it even tougher. Try to obtain better artifacts for its Champions, and research new spells for its Mages. Also, turn a critical eye on the units themselves. Are there certain units that aren't holding their own? A good example of this is a Level 1 or a Level 2 summoned creature. These creatures are reasonably powerful, but they never improve.

Fig. 6-3. This army consists mainly of veterans, but a new unit has been added.

Perhaps you should look into ditching them and replacing them with Level 3 creatures—or replace them with green units that can gain experience levels quickly while traveling with an experienced army, as shown in figure 6-3.

It's absolutely vital that you don't lose too many veterans from your army.

Never underestimate the value of resting an army for several days before sending it to the next combat! Healthy veterans always live longer than wounded ones.

A Note on How the Game is Won

In both single-player and multiplayer games, you'll find that you just can't beat an opponent by sneaking in and taking his Capital. Taking and holding his Capital for a prolonged period eventually defeats an opponent because it takes away his valuable followers and his ability to hire new troops. But taking over the Capital for a short while doesn't disrupt an enemy's plans too much—especially if he has another Capital under his control.

There are two main ways of defeating an enemy faith. The most definitive way is to confront and shatter its best and biggest army. Once a faith's veteran troops are all gone, your own veteran army can handle anything else that the faith sends your way.

The enemy faith can hire new troops if it still has its Capital and outlying structures, but these troops will be relatively green—easy prey for your superior veteran force. Now it's just a matter of taking over the enemy Capital and Great Temple.

The other way to win is to take over the enemy Capital and hold it indefinitely, profiting from its resources as the enemy slowly grows weaker. Even if the enemy faith controls more than one Capital, you eventually win if you control more Capitals than he does. The longer you control more Capitals than your enemies, the more the resource differential between you and your enemies will grow. Eventually, you'll reach a point where you receive so much more gold, ale, and crystals than the enemy that you can muster vast armies and crush his remaining forces.

Regardless of which method you prefer, always remember that the true power of a faith lies not in its Capital, but in its largest veteran armies. You can either crush these armies in head-on confrontation or cut off their resources by taking the enemy Capital; but, regardless of which method you use, the veteran armies are the most significant power in the game.

UNIT COMPARISONS

Chapter 7 has a detailed roster with statistics on every unit in the game. You can use Chapter 7 as a reference text, comparing different units and determining their relative strengths and weaknesses.

It is difficult, however, to get a sense of the big picture when poring over so many unit statistics. Which units are truly best? This is an important question. There are fourteen types of units in the game, such as infantry, cavalry, and scouts. Every faith has a slightly different variant on these fourteen basic archetypes, and some are clearly better than others. It's important to know which faiths' units are best in which categories, so that you'll know which units are best suited for a particular army or for your personal style of play.

The following pages have graphs that depict each faith's variant on the fourteen basic unit types. Each unit is compared to similar units from other faiths to give you a better understanding of the individual variant's strengths and weaknesses. Use this information to build better armies, to understand your opponents, and ultimately to make yourself a better player.

HOW TO READ THE GRAPHS

Graphs are very easy to misinterpret. Read the following sections carefully, so that you don't misinterpret the data in this chapter's unit comparison graphs.

GRAPHS COVER LIMITED STATS

These graphs only compare statistics most relevant to combat; namely, Attack, Defense, Hit Points, and Missile power (generally known as Ranged Attack).

- Attack determines how much damage a unit deals with a successful melee attack.

- Defense protects a unit from a certain percentage of damage from enemy attacks.

- Hit Points measure how much damage a unit can withstand before dying.

- Damage Recovery measures how much time it takes a unit to recover from being hit. Low numbers mean the unit recovers fast, while a high number indicates that the unit is incapacitated for a long time after getting hit. (As with Attack Recovery, low Damage Recovery numbers are better than higher numbers.)

- Speed is a measure of how fast a unit can move around in combat.

- Mana is the total number of mana points a Mage possesses.

- Missile is shorthand for Ranged Attack, which is the amount of damage a unit's long-range attack causes.

> Strength, Dexterity, and Wisdom don't directly come into play in most combat calculations. Instead, they modify units' Attack and Defense ratings. Since the Attack and Defense ratings used in these graphs are the final (modified) ratings, there's not much point in showing ratings for Strength, Dexterity, and Wisdom.
>
> See the beginning of Chapter 7 for more information on the effects of Strength, Dexterity, and Wisdom on Attack and Defense.

UNITS MAY HAVE OTHER ASSETS

All units possess statistics that are less relevant to combat than the ones described here. Also, many units' skills and special abilities—such as Thieves' abilities and each faith's unique spells—aren't shown here. With that in mind, you can't definitively say that one unit is superior to another based on these tables alone.

DON'T JUMP TO CONCLUSIONS!

Graphs can be misleading as they can hide genuine inequalities or make slight differences look like major ones. Take these graphs with a grain of salt and refer to the hard numbers in Chapter 7 if you want an accurate numerical representation of each unit's capabilities.

To put it another way, whenever you see a difference between two units' abilities, just note the difference. Don't assume that it's a huge difference because the discrepancy looks huge. In fact, it may be a fairly trivial discrepancy between the two faiths.

LORDS AND CHAMPIONS

Each faith's Lords are quite similar to its Champions. In fact, Lords and Champions are similar enough in abilities that we won't distinguish between them in the following tables.

WARRIOR LORDS AND CHAMPIONS

This table shows that Air Warrior Champions and Air Warrior Lords are excellent all-around units, featuring great Hit Points and Attack, as well as adequate Defense. With incredible Attack values, Fire and Chaos units show similar attributes, but they have somewhat higher Recovery times. Order's units are particularly well-balanced, while Water is a bit light on Attack and Hit Points. Earth is slow to recover but has excellent Attack and Defense.

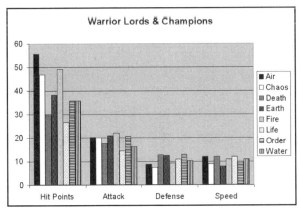

Fig. 6-4. Warrior Lords and Champions

Death's Warriors are surprisingly light on Hit Points, but their strong Defense helps make up for this. Life's Warriors are arguably the least formidable of the lot.

MAGE LORDS AND CHAMPIONS

Mages live and die by their spells, not by their combative skills—so take this table with a "big" grain of salt. Mana and speed are most vital for Mages, as they need to cast spells and move out of the way when enemy melee troops arrive.

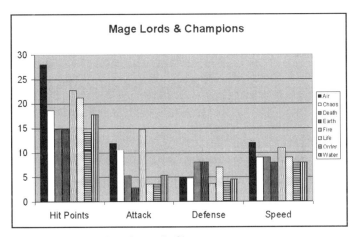

Fig. 6-5. Mage Lords and Champions

Air, Life, and Death win the mana battle, while the other five faiths lag behind. Speed goes to Air and Fire, while the other faiths' Mages are only a notch or two lower.

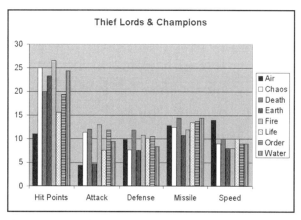

Fig. 6-6. Thief Lords and Champions

THIEF LORDS AND CHAMPIONS

The main combat statistics for Thieves are Missile (Ranged Attack) and various measures of durability. Missile attacks are very close for most Thieves, with Earth as the big loser in this category.

Air's Thief has very low Hit Points, while Earth's has poor Defense. Overall, Earth's Thief is arguably the weakest of the lot.

CONVENTIONAL UNITS

Conventional units are the backbone of most armies. A faith with solid conventional units will have a much easier time early in the game than faiths with weaker conventional units.

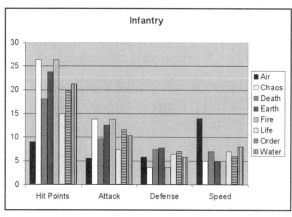

Fig. 6-7. Infantry

INFANTRY

Air infantry's low Hit Points and Attack render it less than ideal, and Life's infantry isn't particularly formidable either. Chaos, Fire, and Earth are the big winners with infantry; Order and Water have solid infantries as well.

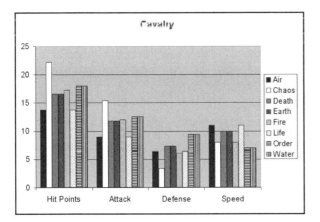

Fig. 6-8. Cavalry

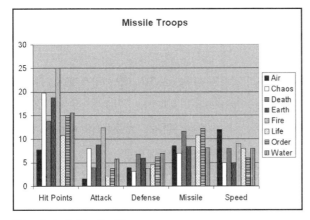

Fig. 6-9. Missile Troops

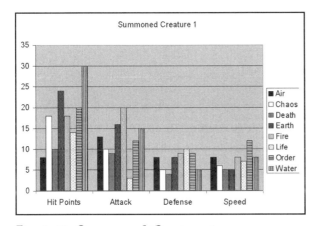

Fig. 6-10. Summoned Creature 1

CAVALRY

Order's and Water's cavalries are identical and excellent, while Fire's and Chaos's receive high marks for their excellent Attack and Hit Points. Air's and Life's cavalries are unremarkable except for their speed, which they share with Death and Earth who are much more combat able.

MISSILE TROOPS

Order and Death come up strong in the important Missile category, while Chaos and Fire get the award for most Hit Points. All these units are good in their own way; some emphasize durability while others are better at all-out attack.

SUMMONED CREATURES

CREATURE 1

Water's first summoned creature is noteworthy for its speed and durability. Life's and Death's offerings are lackluster in spite of Life's creature's excellent Defense.

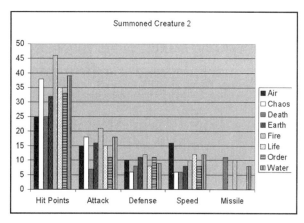

Fig. 6-11. Summoned Creature 2

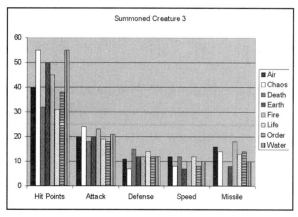

Fig. 6-12. Summoned Creature 3

CREATURE 2

Fire's Demon and Death's Death Shade are remarkable for their missile attacks. The Demon is far and away the most impressive Level 2 creature, while the rest are fairly evenly matched. Each one has unique strengths and weaknesses, but are not completely outclassed by the others.

CREATURE 3

Level 3 summoned creatures are uniformly tough. Many have missile attacks; those that don't have missiles make up for it with great combative skills. Perhaps the most under-powered creature is Life's Pegasus, but even the Pegasus possesses tough Defense and a good mix of Missile and Attack potential.

MISCELLANEOUS UNITS

Miscellaneous units don't see much combat, but here's the lowdown on them anyway. Just bear in mind that these units won't be the mainstay of any army; their combative skills shouldn't be a major issue.

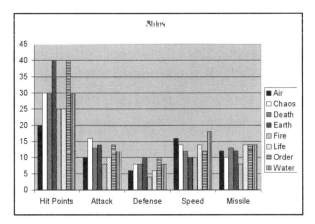

Fig. 6-13. Ships

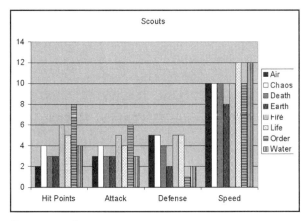

Fig. 6-14. Scouts

SHIPS

Ships run the gamut from tough, war-ready craft to faster, lighter craft with more mobility but less durability. Fire and Earth are the biggest losers in the important Speed category, but Earth makes up for this deficiency with strong combat power. Since Fire hates water, it's not surprising that Fire's ships are the least impressive overall.

SCOUTS

Life and Water have the fastest scouts, and, to some degree, that's all you need to know. Combat stats are more or less irrelevant for scouts, as they are much weaker than even the weakest infantry or cavalry units. Still, for what it's worth, Order's Hound and Fire's Imp are among the best scouts in a fight.

FIGHTING BALKOTH

At some point, you must battle Balkoth. What can you expect when you meet him? What can you do to deal with him? How the heck can you hope to win? There's no easy way to take him out, but it's not impossible.

UNDERSTANDING BALKOTH

Take a quick look at Chapter 7. There you'll find an entry on Balkoth with all of his relevant statistics. Note that Balkoth is considered a Mage Lord. Compare him to a few of the other Mage Lords detailed in Chapter 7.

You'll find that Balkoth is considerably more powerful than other Mage Lords, but not by orders of magnitude. In most areas, he's approximately twice as powerful, if that. Balkoth also has a number of unusual characteristics: he has more Attack and Hit Points than the typical Mage; he also has a Missile attack. In this sense, Balkoth is a bit like a Mage, Warrior, and Thief rolled into one!

But wait—there's more! Notice that Balkoth has a 25- to 50-percent resistance to all faiths except for Death. (Balkoth has a 75-percent resistance to Death itself.) This means that all your magical attacks on Balkoth will have 25 to 50 percent of their damage shaved off. That explains why Balkoth is so darn durable!

Balkoth carries the unique artifact known as Balkoth's Scythe (described fully in Chapter 8). This artifact improves his Attack, Ranged Attack, and Mana; it also allows Balkoth to recover a fraction of his Hit Points by "stealing life" whenever he hits an enemy. Finally, it increases his Capital's crystal production and allows him to cast the damaging World Map spell, Locust, once every turn. All things considered, it's an incredible artifact with awesome powers.

Now you can see why Balkoth is so tough. His base statistics aren't anything to make you run in terror, but his excellent resistance to certain faiths and his awe-inspiring personal artifact turn him into a force to be reckoned with.

Balkoth always travels with a retinue of high-level Death units, primarily consisting of infantry, cavalry, and missile troops. Even without Balkoth, it's a formidable army in its own right.

OPTIMAL TACTICS

What can you do to beat Balkoth? Here are two strategies for finishing him off decisively; both strategies require strong armies and tough troops.

If Balkoth attacks you early in the game—and your armies really aren't up to snuff—you may have to restart and try to build your infrastructure more quickly next time.

Another option is to keep your best armies well away from Balkoth. Allow Balkoth to take over your Capitals and then, when his army leaves, retake them as quickly as possible with fast scouts. If you have multiple Capitals, you can exist like this indefinitely and continue to build up your army. It's sort of a yo-yo effect: Balkoth takes one Capital and goes to take over the next, and you reclaim the one he just captured. Balkoth then takes over the new Capital and goes back to reclaim the one you just recaptured; your scouts then reclaim the second Capital he just left.

It's a pain to have to keep retaking your Capitals, but Balkoth's mega-army can't take over every Capital at once—it has to keep moving. This allows you to keep retaking your Capitals and to hold your ground indefinitely.

THE MAGES' GAMBIT

The first—and perhaps easiest—way of defeating Balkoth is to use Mages to pick away at him. Balkoth is deadly at all ranges but tends not to fling too many spells until his army is within moderate range. By attacking him with Mage spells at the very beginning of combat, you may be able to kill him before he has the opportunity to destroy your forces.

This technique requires a few reasonably high-level Mages, but does not require you to research many new spells. Any faith and leader type should be able to pursue this strategy.

Here's the procedure:

1. Attack Balkoth's army with an army of several melee troops and a couple high-level Mages. The melee troops are just a distraction; the Mages are the real force in this army.

2. Have the Mages immediately cast low-level, direct-damage spells on Balkoth. Every faith has a spell like this. For Air, it's Lightning; for Earth, it's Rocksling; for Fire, it's Flame Dart. Chaos has spells that cause damage but also increase the target's combat abilities; these also will work. Cast these spells as quickly and as soon as possible. Target Balkoth exclusively; pause the game after every spell to aim another spell at Balkoth.

3. If you have enough high-level Mages in your group, you can actually kill Balkoth outright before coming into contact with his army. If your Mages run out of mana and Balkoth is still alive, have your army run. Use melee troops to block his Death units, so that your Mages can run to safety. (This may not always be possible, but you should at least try to escape.) Try to keep your troops away from Balkoth, so that he can't use his vampiric attacks to regain health.

4. If Balkoth survives, attack him with another army, including Mages during the same turn (or wait until the next turn and attack again with any Mages that survived). Repeat the whole process again. The first attack should have weakened Balkoth; you should have a better chance of killing him the second time around.

That's the essence of this strategy. Balkoth only sustains incremental damage from your Mages' low-level spells, but then again, he takes very little damage from everything. Cheap spells, therefore, are the most efficient way of killing Balkoth, as your Mages can cast tons of 'em—and every point of damage counts.

This strategy requires you to ignore Balkoth's army completely. Once Balkoth is dead, you win—regardless of whether his army lives or dies.

> **This strategy is easiest if you have a Mage Lord and another Lord under your control. Your powerful Mage Lord can cast spells on Balkoth, and if the Mage Lord dies in the fray, you still win the game because your other Lord survived (provided that you kill Balkoth, of course).**

FULL-BORE ATTACKS

The second method is simple in theory but difficult in practice. It essentially involves amassing several large armies and throwing them all at Balkoth and company in rapid succession. Ideally, all armies should attack one after the other during the same turn. With this kind of attack, Balkoth usually runs out of mana after fighting the first army, rendering him less effective in subsequent battles.

When your armies attack, have them ignore Balkoth and concentrate on eliminating individual Death units. Whittle down Balkoth's army slowly but surely. Eventually, you may be able to reduce his army until it consists of Balkoth alone. At that point, you can rush him with hordes of melee and missile troops.

This technique works best if you have lots of resources in stock and if you fight Balkoth on your home turf, right next to one of your Capitals. That way you can hire several mercenary armies (or summon new creatures) after your first waves of armies have been defeated. Hopefully, the first armies can soften up Balkoth's troops to the point where your mercenaries or newly summoned creatures can finish them off.

Note that most Level 3 summoned creatures have a certain percentage of resistance to Death attacks; they're excellent additions to armies fighting Balkoth.

Good luck!

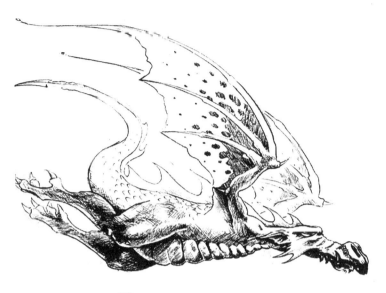

CHAPTER

COMBAT UNITS OF URAK

This chapter is a complete roster of every unit in the game. All units are ranked in a number of significant categories ranging from Movement to Hit Points to Maintenance cost. In the case of units capable of advancing in level, tables show their progressive increases in various attributes as their level increases.

Here's a master list of the statistics for each unit. Note that not every unit qualifies for every statistic. (For example, non-Mages don't have a Mana rating, and units without a missile attack don't have a Missile or Missile Range rating.)

- Exp: Experience is a series of numbers representing the experience point thresholds necessary to advance from one level to the next. If a unit has a Level 2 Exp rating of 200, it needs 200 experience points to reach the second level.

- Str, Dex, Wis: Strength, Dexterity, and Wisdom are primary attributes that influence many aspects of the game. (See note below.)

- H.P.: Hit Points are a measure of how much damage a unit can sustain.

- Att: Attack is a measure of how much damage a unit deals with each melee attack. (See note below.)

- Def: Defense is a measure of how well-protected the unit is. Units with higher Defense sustain less damage. (See note below.)

- Hit Rec: Hit Recovery measures how quickly the unit can "recover" from an attack and initiate a new attack. Lower numbers are better!

- Dam Rec: Damage Recovery measures how quickly a unit recovers from being hit. Again, lower numbers are better.

- Mana: The unit's maximum mana value; only Mages can have this attribute.

- Missile: Otherwise known as Ranged Attack, this statistic measures how much damage a unit's missiles cause.

- Movement: A measure of the unit's overland speed.

- Sight: How far a unit can see on the overland map.

- Stealth: How much noise a unit makes. This comes into play when a Thief tries to hide a unit. Lower numbers, again, are better!

- Missile Range: The distance a missile unit's missiles travel.

- Cost: The initial cost to train a unit.

- Maintenance: The cost of maintaining a unit per turn.

- Hit Point Recovery: Speed at which units recover Hit Points. This attribute is expressed as three values separated by slashes. The first number expresses the number of Hit Points recovered per turn while the unit is inside a structure; the second shows how many Hit Points are recovered per turn outside a structure. The third number expresses how many Hit Points are recovered during a turn in which the unit moves, regardless of whether the unit ends the turn indoors or outdoors.

Every unit has a base Attack value and a base Defense value (also known as Armor). Strength and Dexterity modify these base values, respectively; as Strength and Dexterity rise, so do the modifiers applied to the base Attack and Defense values.

The Attack and Defense ratings listed in this chapter are not the units' base values. Rather, they're modified "end-result" values that already have had Strength and Dexterity bonuses applied to them. This makes it easier for you to see each unit's true strengths and weaknesses, rather than forcing you to calculate modified values. Of course, this also reduces the importance of Strength and Dexterity because you can see these attributes' influence directly. We list them here anyway, just to satiate the curious.

Ranged Attack ("Missile" in this chapter) and Mana are also modified by other attributes. Dexterity modifies Ranged Attack, and Wisdom modifies Mana. But again, the values presented in this chapter are final modified values. No math is required! We just thought you might like to know how Strength, Dexterity, and Wisdom play a role in determining other important values.

AIR UNITS

CHAMPIONS AND LORDS

STORM WARLORD (AIR WARRIOR LORD)

	Exp	Str	Dex	Wis	H.P.	Att	Def	Hit Rec	Dam Rec
Level 1	0	13	6	5	28	13	5	8	0
Level 2	236	15	6	5	36	15	5	7	0
Level 3	769	16	6	5	42	17	6	6	0
Level 4	1,789	17	7	6	48	18	6	5	0
Level 5	3,233	18	8	6	52	20	7	4	0
Level 6	5,241	18	9	6	56	20	8	4	0
Level 7	7,509	18	10	7	60	21	10	3	0
Level 8	10,127	19	11	7	64	22	10	3	0
Level 9	13,122	19	11	7	66	23	11	3	0
Level 10	16,608	19	12	8	68	23	12	2	0
Level 11	20,334	20	12	9	72	25	13	2	0
Level 12	24,633	21	12	10	76	27	13	1	0

Movement: 24

Sight: 4

Stealth: 11

Hit Point Recovery: 4/2/0

STORM LORD (AIR MAGE LORD)

	Exp	Str	Dex	Wis	H.P.	Att	Def	Hit Rec	Dam Rec	Mana
Level 1	0	10	7	10	18	8	2	10	2	7
Level 2	564	11	7	12	20	9	2	9	2	9
Level 3	1,337	11	8	14	22	9	2	9	2	11
Level 4	2,304	11	8	16	24	9	3	8	2	13
Level 5	3,474	12	9	18	26	11	4	8	1	15
Level 6	4,875	12	9	20	28	11	4	7	1	17
Level 7	6,478	13	10	22	30	12	6	7	1	19
Level 8	8,310	13	10	24	32	13	6	6	0	21
Level 9	10,416	14	11	27	34	14	6	6	0	24
Level 10	12,961	14	11	30	34	14	7	6	0	27
Level 11	15,692	15	12	33	34	16	9	5	0	30
Level 12	18,703	16	12	36	34	17	9	5	0	33

Movement: 24

Sight: 4

Stealth: 10

Hit Point Recovery: 4/2/0

FAERIE LORD (AIR THIEF LORD)

	Exp	Str	Dex	Wis	H.P.	Att	Def	Hit Rec	Dam Rec	Missile
Level 1	0	4	13	5	8	1	5	21	1	7
Level 2	309	4	14	5	9	2	5	20	0	7
Level 3	784	4	15	5	9	3	7	19	0	9
Level 4	1,337	5	16	6	10	3	8	18	0	11
Level 5	2,411	5	17	6	10	4	8	17	0	11
Level 6	3,942	5	18	6	11	4	9	17	0	13
Level 7	5,529	5	19	7	11	5	11	16	0	14
Level 8	8,056	6	20	7	12	5	11	16	0	15
Level 9	11,702	6	20	7	12	6	12	15	0	15
Level 10	15,859	6	21	8	13	6	13	15	0	17
Level 11	21,196	7	21	9	14	7	14	14	0	17
Level 12	27,374	7	22	10	14	7	15	14	0	18

Missile Range: 12

Movement: 28

Sight: 7

Stealth: 1

Hit Point Recovery: 4/2/0

STORM WARRIOR (AIR WARRIOR CHAMPION)

	Exp	Str	Dex	Wis	H.P.	Att	Def	Hit Rec	Dam Rec
Level 1	0	12	4	4	24	12	4	8	0
Level 2	236	14	4	4	32	14	4	7	0
Level 3	769	15	4	4	38	16	5	6	0
Level 4	1,789	16	5	5	44	17	5	5	0
Level 5	3,233	17	6	5	48	19	6	4	0
Level 6	5,241	17	7	5	52	19	6	4	0
Level 7	7,509	17	8	6	56	20	7	3	0
Level 8	10,127	18	9	6	60	21	8	3	0
Level 9	13,122	18	9	6	62	22	9	3	0
Level 10	16,608	18	10	7	64	22	10	2	0

Movement: 20

Sight: 3

Stealth: 12

Cost: 55 Ale, 18 Gold

Maintenance: 1 Ale

Hit Point Recovery: 4/2/0

STORM SORCERER (AIR MAGE CHAMPION)

	Exp	Str	Dex	Wis	H.P.	Att	Def	Hit Rec	Dam Rec	Mana
Level 1	0	10	5	8	16	8	1	10	2	5
Level 2	564	11	5	10	18	9	1	9	2	7
Level 3	1,337	11	6	12	20	9	1	9	2	9
Level 4	2,304	11	6	14	22	9	2	8	2	11
Level 5	3,474	12	7	16	24	11	2	8	1	13
Level 6	4,875	12	7	18	26	11	2	7	1	15
Level 7	6,478	13	8	20	28	12	3	7	1	17
Level 8	8,310	13	8	22	30	13	3	6	0	19
Level 9	10,416	14	9	25	32	14	4	6	0	22
Level 10	12,961	14	9	28	32	14	5	6	0	25

Movement: 20

Sight: 3

Stealth: 11

Cost: 17 Ale, 52 Crystals

Maintenance: 1 Crystal

Hit Point Recovery: 4/2/0

FAERIE THIEF (AIR THIEF CHAMPION)

	Exp	Str	Dex	Wis	H.P.	Att	Def	Hit Rec	Dam Rec	Missile
Level 1	0	3	12	4	5	1	3	21	1	6
Level 2	309	3	13	4	6	2	4	20	0	7
Level 3	784	3	14	4	6	3	5	19	0	8
Level 4	1,337	4	15	5	7	3	6	18	0	10
Level 5	2,411	4	16	5	7	4	7	17	0	11
Level 6	3,942	4	17	5	8	4	7	17	0	12
Level 7	5,529	4	18	6	8	5	9	16	0	13
Level 8	8,056	5	19	6	9	5	10	16	0	15
Level 9	11,702	5	19	6	9	6	11	15	0	15
Level 10	15,859	5	20	7	10	6	11	15	0	16

Missile Range: 12

Movement: 24

Sight: 6

Stealth: 2

Cost: 14 Crystals, 41 Gold

Maintenance: 1 Gold

Hit Point Recovery: 4/2/0

CONVENTIONAL UNITS

EAGLES (AIR INFANTRY)

	Exp	Str	Dex	Wis	H.P.	Att	Def	Hit Rec	Dam Rec
Level 1	0	6	14	5	7	4	4	8	10
Level 2	393	7	15	5	8	5	5	8	9
Level 3	828	8	16	5	9	6	6	8	9
Level 4	1,569	8	17	6	10	6	6	8	8
Level 5	2,292	9	18	6	11	7	8	8	8

Movement: 28

Sight: 5

Stealth: 3

Cost: 32 Ale, 11 Gold

Maintenance: 1 Ale

Hit Point Recovery: 3/3/2

WINDRIDERS (AIR CAVALRY)

	Exp	Str	Dex	Wis	H.P.	Att	Def	Hit Rec	Dam Rec
Level 1	0	7	9	6	9	6	3	10	8
Level 2	223	7	10	6	12	7	5	10	8
Level 3	569	8	11	6	14	9	6	9	7
Level 4	1,251	9	12	7	16	11	8	9	7
Level 5	2,433	9	13	7	18	12	10	8	6

Movement: 22

Sight: 3

Stealth: 10

Cost: 21 Ale, 7 Gold

Maintenance: 1 Ale

Hit Point Recovery: 3/3/1

FAE SLINGERS (AIR MISSILE TROOPS)

	Exp	Str	Dex	Wis	H.P.	Att	Def	Hit Rec	Dam Rec	Missile
Level 1	0	3	10	3	5	1	2	18	12	5
Level 2	288	3	12	4	7	1	3	16	11	7
Level 3	801	4	13	4	8	2	4	14	11	9
Level 4	1,921	4	14	5	9	2	5	12	11	10
Level 5	3,239	5	15	5	10	2	6	11	10	12

Missile Range: 10

Movement: 24

Sight: 4

Stealth: 3

Cost: 11 Crystals, 33 Gold

Maintenance: 1 Gold

Hit Point Recovery: 3/3/1

SUMMONED UNITS

WILL O' WISP

Str	Dex	Wis	H.P.	Att	Def	Hit Rec	Dam Rec
3	19	8	8	13	8	15	3

Movement: 16

Sight: 2

Stealth: 3

Cost: 11 Ale, 32 Crystals

Maintenance: 1 Crystal

Hit Point Recovery: 4/2/0

25 percent resistance to Air magic.

AIR ELEMENTAL

Str	Dex	Wis	H.P.	Att	Def	Hit Rec	Dam Rec
6	20	4	25	15	10	10	4

Movement: 32

Sight: 2

Stealth: 2

Cost: 24 Ale, 71 Crystals

Maintenance: 3 Crystals

Hit Point Recovery: 4/2/0

50 percent resistance to Air magic, 25 percent resistance to Chaos and Life magic.

THUNDER DRAKE

Str	Dex	Wis	H.P.	Att	Def	Hit Rec	Dam Rec	Missile
19	8	10	40	20	11	14	2	16

Missile Range: 10

Movement: 24

Sight: 4

Stealth: 12

Cost: 85 Ale, 255 Crystals

Maintenance: 8 Crystals

Hit Point Recovery: 4/2/0

100 percent resistance to Air magic; 75 percent resistance to Chaos and Life magic; 50 percent resistance to Fire and Water magic; 25 percent resistance to Death, Earth, and Order magic.

MISCELLANEOUS UNITS

DRAGONFLY (AIR SCOUT)

Str	Dex	Wis	H.P.	Att	Def	Hit Rec	Dam Rec
1	10	3	2	3	5	12	12

Movement: 20

Sight: 4

Stealth: 2

Cost: 4 Ale, 4 Crystals, 11 Gold

Maintenance: 1 Gold

Hit Point Recovery: 4/2/0

WINDJAMMER (AIR SHIP)

Str	Dex	Wis	H.P.	Att	Def	Hit Rec	Dam Rec	Missile
0	0	0	20	10	6	40	10	12

Missile Range: 12

Movement: 32

Sight: 5

Stealth: 12

Cost: 9 Ale, 9 Crystals, 28 Gold

Maintenance: 1 Ale, 1 Gold

Hit Point Recovery: 4/2/0

CHAOS UNITS

CHAMPIONS AND LORDS

BEAST LORD (CHAOS WARRIOR LORD)

	Exp	Str	Dex	Wis	H.P.	Att	Def	Hit Rec	Dam Rec
Level 1	0	12	8	5	22	14	3	14	2
Level 2	207	13	9	5	30	15	4	14	2
Level 3	577	15	10	5	38	18	5	13	1
Level 4	1,411	16	10	6	42	20	6	12	1
Level 5	2,801	17	11	6	46	21	6	11	0
Level 6	4,546	17	11	6	48	21	7	11	0
Level 7	6,481	17	12	7	50	21	8	11	0
Level 8	8,563	17	12	7	54	21	9	10	0
Level 9	11,064	17	12	7	58	21	9	10	0
Level 10	13,824	17	12	8	58	21	10	10	0
Level 11	16,687	18	13	9	58	23	11	9	0
Level 12	20,094	18	14	10	58	24	12	9	0

Movement: 18

Sight: 3

Stealth: 6

Hit Point Recovery: 4/2/0

SHAMAN LORD (CHAOS MAGE LORD)

	Exp	Str	Dex	Wis	H.P.	Att	Def	Hit Rec	Dam Rec	Mana
Level 1	0	9	9	9	12	5	2	18	2	6
Level 2	446	10	10	10	14	7	3	17	2	7
Level 3	1,005	11	11	11	16	9	3	16	2	8
Level 4	1,687	11	11	13	18	10	3	15	1	10
Level 5	2,569	11	11	15	18	10	4	15	1	12
Level 6	3,639	12	12	17	18	11	5	15	0	14
Level 7	4,943	12	12	19	20	12	5	14	0	16
Level 8	6,456	12	12	21	20	12	5	14	0	18
Level 9	8,153	12	13	23	22	12	7	13	0	20
Level 10	10,127	13	13	25	22	13	7	13	0	22
Level 11	12,326	13	14	27	22	13	7	13	0	24
Level 12	14,708	13	14	29	22	13	7	13	0	26

Movement: 18

Sight: 4

Stealth: 6

Hit Point Recovery: 4/2/0

HUNTRESS LORD (CHAOS THIEF LORD)

	Exp	Str	Dex	Wis	H.P.	Att	Def	Hit Rec	Dam Rec	Missile
Level 1	0	9	11	5	15	5	3	14	1	6
Level 2	120	9	12	5	19	6	5	13	1	9
Level 3	336	10	13	5	23	8	6	12	1	11
Level 4	850	10	14	6	25	9	7	11	0	11
Level 5	1,831	11	14	6	26	11	7	11	0	11
Level 6	2,949	11	15	6	27	12	8	10	0	13
Level 7	4,258	12	15	7	27	13	8	10	0	13
Level 8	5,682	12	16	7	27	13	9	10	0	14
Level 9	7,464	12	16	7	27	13	9	9	0	15
Level 10	10,079	13	17	8	27	15	10	9	0	15
Level 11	13,439	13	17	9	28	15	10	9	0	16
Level 12	17,669	13	17	10	29	16	10	9	0	16

Missile Range: 6

Movement: 18

Sight: 4

Stealth: 3

Hit Point Recovery: 4/2/0

BEAST RIDER (CHAOS WARRIOR CHAMPION)

	Exp	Str	Dex	Wis	H.P.	Att	Def	Hit Rec	Dam Rec
Level 1	0	11	8	4	18	13	2	14	2
Level 2	207	12	9	4	26	14	3	14	2
Level 3	577	14	10	4	34	17	4	13	1
Level 4	1,411	15	10	5	38	19	5	12	1
Level 5	2,801	16	11	5	42	20	5	11	0
Level 6	4,546	16	11	5	44	20	6	11	0
Level 7	6,481	16	12	6	46	20	7	11	0
Level 8	8,563	16	12	6	50	20	8	10	0
Level 9	11,064	16	12	6	54	20	8	10	0
Level 10	13,824	16	12	7	54	20	9	10	0

Movement: 14

Sight: 2

Stealth: 7

Cost: 45 Ale, 15 Gold

Maintenance: 1 Ale

Hit Point Recovery: 4/2/0

SHAMAN (CHAOS MAGE CHAMPION)

	Exp	Str	Dex	Wis	H.P.	Att	Def	Hit Rec	Dam Rec	Mana
Level 1	0	9	9	9	10	5	1	18	2	6
Level 2	446	10	10	10	12	7	2	17	2	7
Level 3	1,005	11	11	11	14	9	2	16	2	8
Level 4	1,687	11	11	13	16	10	2	15	1	10
Level 5	2,569	11	11	15	16	10	3	15	1	12
Level 6	3,639	12	12	17	16	11	4	15	0	14
Level 7	4,943	12	12	19	18	12	4	14	0	16
Level 8	6,456	12	12	21	18	12	4	14	0	18
Level 9	8,153	12	13	23	20	12	6	13	0	20
Level 10	10,127	13	13	25	20	13	6	13	0	22

Movement: 14

Sight: 3

Stealth: 7

Cost: 12 Ale, 37 Crystals

Maintenance: 1 Crystal

Hit Point Recovery: 4/2/0

Huntress (Chaos Thief Champion)

	Exp	Str	Dex	Wis	H.P.	Att	Def	Hit Rec	Dam Rec	Missile
Level 1	0	9	10	4	12	5	2	14	1	6
Level 2	120	9	11	4	16	6	3	13	1	8
Level 3	336	10	12	4	20	8	4	12	1	10
Level 4	850	10	13	5	22	9	6	11	0	11
Level 5	1,831	11	13	5	23	11	6	11	0	11
Level 6	2,949	11	14	5	24	12	6	10	0	12
Level 7	4,258	12	14	6	24	13	6	10	0	12
Level 8	5,682	12	15	6	24	13	7	10	0	13
Level 9	7,464	12	15	6	24	13	7	9	0	14
Level 10	10,079	13	16	7	24	15	9	9	0	15

Missile Range: 6

Movement: 14

Sight: 3

Stealth: 4

Cost: 10 Crystals, 29 Gold

Maintenance: 1 Gold

Hit Point Recovery: 4/2/0

CONVENTIONAL UNITS

BERSERKERS (CHAOS INFANTRY)

	Exp	Str	Dex	Wis	H.P.	Att	Def	Hit Rec	Dam Rec
Level 1	0	10	8	4	16	10	2	12	6
Level 2	368	11	9	4	24	13	3	11	6
Level 3	1,278	12	9	4	28	14	3	10	5
Level 4	2,743	13	10	5	32	15	5	10	4
Level 5	4,772	14	11	5	32	17	5	10	3

Movement: 10

Sight: 1

Stealth: 7

Cost: 48 Ale, 16 Gold

Maintenance: 1 Ale

Hit Point Recovery: 4/4/2

RAIDERS (CHAOS CAVALRY)

	Exp	Str	Dex	Wis	H.P.	Att	Def	Hit Rec	Dam Rec
Level 1	0	10	8	4	14	11	2	15	6
Level 2	407	12	8	4	19	15	2	13	6
Level 3	1,377	13	9	4	24	16	3	12	5
Level 4	2,898	14	10	5	26	17	5	11	4
Level 5	4,741	14	10	5	28	18	5	10	3

Movement: 16

Sight: 1

Stealth: 11

Cost: 51 Ale, 17 Gold

Maintenance: 1 Ale

Hit Point Recovery: 3/3/1

STICKTHROWERS (CHAOS MISSILE TROOPS)

	Exp	Str	Dex	Wis	H.P.	Att	Def	Hit Rec	Dam Rec	Missile
Level 1	0	9	9	3	12	4	2	13	6	4
Level 2	228	10	10	4	18	7	3	12	5	6
Level 3	737	11	11	4	21	9	3	11	4	7
Level 4	1,480	12	11	5	24	10	3	10	3	8
Level 5	2,436	12	12	5	24	10	5	9	3	10

Missile Range: 7

Movement: 10

Sight: 1

Stealth: 6

Cost: 9 Crystals, 27 Gold

Maintenance: 1 Gold

Hit Point Recovery: 3/3/1

SUMMONED UNITS

GOBLINS

Str	Dex	Wis	H.P.	Att	Def	Hit Rec	Dam Rec
11	8	4	18	10	5	10	8

Movement: 12

Sight: 2

Stealth: 9

Cost: 12 Ale, 35 Crystals

Maintenance: 1 Crystal

Hit Point Recovery: 4/2/0

25 percent resistance to Chaos magic.

OGRE

Str	Dex	Wis	H.P.	Att	Def	Hit Rec	Dam Rec
16	5	2	38	18	6	21	2

Movement: 12

Sight: 1

Stealth: 9

Cost: 22 Ale, 65 Crystals

Maintenance: 3 Crystals

Hit Point Recovery: 4/2/0

50 percent resistance to Chaos magic, 25 percent resistance to Air and Fire magic.

CYCLOPS

Str	Dex	Wis	H.P.	Att	Def	Hit Rec	Dam Rec	Missile
20	6	4	55	12	7	4	0	14

Missile Range: 9

Movement: 16

Sight: 3

Stealth: 12

Cost: 68 Ale, 203 Crystals

Maintenance: 5 Crystals

Hit Point Recovery: 4/2/0

75 percent resistance to Chaos magic, 50 percent resistance to Air and Fire magic, 25 percent resistance to Death and Life magic.

MISCELLANEOUS UNITS

WILD CAT (CHAOS SCOUT)

Str	Dex	Wis	H.P.	Att	Def	Hit Rec	Dam Rec
3	12	5	4	4	5	10	10

Movement: 20

Sight: 4

Stealth: 2

Cost: 2 Ale, 2 Crystals, 7 Gold

Maintenance: 1 Gold

Hit Point Recovery: 4/2/0

LONGBOAT (CHAOS SHIP)

Str	Dex	Wis	H.P.	Att	Def	Hit Rec	Dam Rec	Missile
0	0	0	30	16	8	30	6	10

Missile Range: 14

Movement: 28

Sight: 5

Stealth: 12

Cost: 15 Ale, 15 Crystals, 46 Gold

Maintenance: 1 Ale, 1 Gold

Hit Point Recovery: 4/2/0

DEATH UNITS

CHAMPIONS AND LORDS

SPECIAL: BALKOTH

	Exp	Str	Dex	Wis	H.P.	Att	Def	Hit Rec	Dam Rec	Missile	Mana
Level 1	0	9	11	12	16	7	6	12	2	3	11
Level 2	999	9	12	14	17	7	7	11	2	4	13
Level 3	2,172	10	13	16	18	8	8	11	2	5	15
Level 4	3,666	10	14	18	19	8	8	10	1	5	17
Level 5	5,323	10	15	20	20	9	10	10	1	6	19
Level 6	7,557	11	16	22	21	10	11	9	1	7	21
Level 7	9,996	11	17	24	22	10	11	9	0	7	23
Level 8	13,467	11	17	26	23	11	12	8	0	7	25
Level 9	17,255	12	18	29	23	12	13	8	0	8	28
Level 10	21,488	12	18	32	24	12	13	7	0	8	31
Level 11	25,970	13	19	35	24	14	15	7	0	9	34
Level 12	31,133	13	19	38	24	14	15	7	0	9	37

Missile Range: 18

Movement: 24

Sight: 5

Stealth: 8

Hit Point Recovery: 3/1/0

75 percent resistance to Death magic; 50 percent resistance to Earth and Fire magic; 25 percent resistance to Air, Chaos, Life, Order, and Water magic. Balkoth begins with Death artifact Balkoth's Scythe.

DARK WARLORD (DEATH WARRIOR LORD)

	Exp	Str	Dex	Wis	H.P.	Att	Def	Hit Rec	Dam Rec
Level 1	0	11	10	7	16	11	7	12	0
Level 2	203	11	11	7	19	12	8	11	0
Level 3	481	12	12	7	22	14	10	10	0
Level 4	1,037	12	13	8	25	15	12	9	0
Level 5	2,012	13	13	8	28	17	12	8	0
Level 6	3,250	13	14	8	30	17	13	8	0
Level 7	4,763	14	14	9	32	19	13	8	0
Level 8	6,385	14	15	9	34	19	14	8	0
Level 9	8,575	15	15	9	36	21	15	8	0
Level 10	11,354	15	16	10	38	21	16	8	0
Level 11	14,861	16	17	11	40	23	16	7	0
Level 12	19,183	17	18	12	40	24	18	7	0

Movement: 24

Sight: 4

Stealth: 5

Hit Point Recovery: 1/1/0

NECROMANCER LORD (DEATH MAGE LORD)

	Exp	Str	Dex	Wis	H.P.	Att	Def	Hit Rec	Dam Rec	Mana
Level 1	0	7	10	10	10	3	4	20	0	7
Level 2	455	7	11	12	11	3	4	19	0	9
Level 3	1,055	8	12	14	12	3	5	19	0	11
Level 4	1,823	8	13	16	13	3	6	18	0	13
Level 5	2,745	8	14	18	14	4	7	18	0	15
Level 6	3,876	9	15	20	15	5	8	17	0	17
Level 7	5,173	9	16	22	16	5	9	17	0	19
Level 8	6,703	9	16	24	17	6	10	16	0	21
Level 9	8,487	10	17	27	17	7	10	16	0	24
Level 10	10,494	10	17	30	18	7	10	15	0	27
Level 11	12,649	11	18	33	18	9	12	15	0	30
Level 12	15,141	11	18	36	18	9	12	15	0	33

Movement: 18

Sight: 5

Stealth: 3

Hit Point Recovery: 1/1/0

ASSASSIN LORD (DEATH THIEF LORD)

	Exp	Str	Dex	Wis	H.P.	Att	Def	Hit Rec	Dam Rec	Missile
Level 1	0	8	13	8	13	5	7	11	1	7
Level 2	199	8	14	8	15	6	7	11	0	9
Level 3	787	9	15	8	17	9	9	10	0	11
Level 4	1,629	9	16	9	18	10	10	10	0	13
Level 5	3,006	9	17	9	19	12	11	10	0	14
Level 6	5,770	10	17	9	20	13	11	9	0	14
Level 7	8,929	10	18	10	21	13	13	9	0	16
Level 8	12,704	10	18	10	22	14	13	9	0	16
Level 9	16,760	11	19	10	23	15	15	8	0	17
Level 10	23,752	11	19	11	23	15	15	8	0	18
Level 11	31,009	11	20	12	24	16	15	8	0	18
Level 12	39,043	12	21	13	25	17	17	8	0	20

Missile Range: 6

Movement: 20

Sight: 7

Stealth: 2

Hit Point Recovery: 1/1/0

DARK WARRIOR (DEATH WARRIOR CHAMPION)

	Exp	Str	Dex	Wis	H.P.	Att	Def	Hit Rec	Dam Rec
Level 1	0	10	10	7	12	10	6	12	2
Level 2	203	10	11	7	15	11	7	11	2
Level 3	481	11	12	7	18	13	9	10	1
Level 4	1,037	11	13	8	21	14	11	9	1
Level 5	2,012	12	13	8	24	16	11	8	1
Level 6	3,250	12	14	8	26	16	12	8	1
Level 7	4,763	13	14	9	28	18	12	8	1
Level 8	6,385	13	15	9	30	18	13	8	0
Level 9	8,575	14	15	9	32	20	14	8	0
Level 10	11,354	14	16	10	34	20	15	8	0

Movement: 20

Sight: 3

Stealth: 6

Cost: 32 Ale, 11 Gold

Maintenance: 1 Ale

Hit Point Recovery: 1/1/0

NECROMANCER (DEATH MAGE CHAMPION)

	Exp	Str	Dex	Wis	H.P.	Att	Def	Hit Rec	Dam Rec	Mana
Level 1	0	6	10	12	8	3	3	20	0	7
Level 2	455	6	11	14	9	3	3	19	0	9
Level 3	1,055	7	12	16	10	3	4	19	0	11
Level 4	1,823	7	13	18	11	3	5	18	0	13
Level 5	2,745	7	14	20	12	4	6	18	0	15
Level 6	3,876	8	15	22	13	4	7	17	0	17
Level 7	5,173	8	16	24	14	4	8	17	0	19
Level 8	6,703	8	16	26	15	5	9	16	0	21
Level 9	8,487	9	17	29	15	6	9	16	0	24
Level 10	10,494	9	17	32	16	6	9	15	0	27

Movement: 14

Sight: 4

Stealth: 4

Cost: 14 Ale, 42 Crystals

Maintenance: 1 Crystal

Hit Point Recovery: 1/1/0

ASSASSIN (DEATH THIEF CHAMPION)

	Exp	Str	Dex	Wis	H.P.	Att	Def	Hit Rec	Dam Rec	Missile
Level 1	0	8	12	8	10	5	5	11	1	6
Level 2	199	8	13	8	12	6	6	11	0	9
Level 3	787	9	14	8	14	9	7	10	0	10
Level 4	1,629	9	15	9	15	10	8	10	0	12
Level 5	3,006	9	16	9	16	12	10	10	0	14
Level 6	5,770	10	16	9	17	13	10	9	0	14
Level 7	8,929	10	17	10	18	13	11	9	0	15
Level 8	12,704	10	17	10	19	14	11	9	0	15
Level 9	16,760	11	18	10	20	15	13	8	0	16
Level 10	23,752	11	18	11	20	15	13	8	0	17

Missile Range: 6

Movement: 16

Sight: 6

Stealth: 3

Cost: 17 Crystals, 50 Gold

Maintenance: 1 Gold

Hit Point Recovery: 1/1/0

CONVENTIONAL UNITS

DARK HALBERDIERS (DEATH INFANTRY)

	Exp	Str	Dex	Wis	H.P.	Att	Def	Hit Rec	Dam Rec
Level 1	0	8	9	6	12	6	4	12	7
Level 2	278	9	10	6	15	8	6	11	6
Level 3	820	10	11	6	18	10	7	11	6
Level 4	1,573	10	12	7	21	11	9	10	5
Level 5	3,112	11	13	7	24	13	11	9	5

Movement: 14

Sight: 1

Stealth: 4

Cost: 29 Ale, 10 Gold

Maintenance: 1 Ale

Hit Point Recovery: 3/2/1

DARK HORSEMEN (DEATH CAVALRY)

	Exp	Str	Dex	Wis	H.P.	Att	Def	Hit Rec	Dam Rec
Level 1	0	9	9	6	11	8	4	12	7
Level 2	306	10	10	6	14	10	6	12	7
Level 3	954	10	11	6	17	12	7	11	6
Level 4	1,852	11	12	7	19	14	9	10	5
Level 5	3,882	11	13	7	22	15	11	9	5

Movement: 20

Sight: 2

Stealth: 10

Cost: 36 Ale, 12 Gold

Maintenance: 1 Ale

Hit Point Recovery: 3/1/1

DARK JAVELINS (DEATH MISSILE TROOPS)

	Exp	Str	Dex	Wis	H.P.	Att	Def	Hit Rec	Dam Rec	Missile
Level 1	0	8	10	6	9	2	4	19	8	8
Level 2	426	8	11	7	12	2	5	17	7	9
Level 3	1,233	9	12	7	14	4	7	16	7	12
Level 4	2,917	9	13	8	16	5	9	14	6	14
Level 5	7,133	10	14	8	18	7	9	13	6	15

Missile Range: 9
Movement: 16
Sight: 3
Stealth: 4
Cost: 15 Crystals, 44 Gold
Maintenance: 1 Gold
Hit Point Recovery: 1/1/0

SUMMONED UNITS

SKELETONS

Str	Dex	Wis	H.P.	Att	Def	Hit Rec	Dam Rec
10	3	0	10	9	4	18	4

Movement: 10
Sight: 1
Stealth: 9
Cost: 8 Ale, 24 Crystals
Maintenance: 1 Crystal
Hit Point Recovery: 0/0/0

25 percent resistance to Death magic.

DEATH SHADE

Str	Dex	Wis	H.P.	Att	Def	Hit Rec	Dam Rec	Missile
8	8	8	25	7	8	15	4	11

Missile Range: 10

Movement: 12

Sight: 2

Stealth: 3

Cost: 22 Ale, 67 Crystals

Maintenance: 3 Crystals

Hit Point Recovery: 0/0/0

50 percent resistance to Death magic; 25 percent resistance to Earth and Fire magic.

VAMPIRE

Str	Dex	Wis	H.P.	Att	Def	Hit Rec	Dam Rec
16	13	8	32	18	15	12	4

Movement: 24

Sight: 5

Stealth: 3

Cost: 57 Ale, 172 Crystals

Maintenance: 5 Crystals

Hit Point Recovery: 0/0/0

75 percent resistance to Death magic; 50 percent resistance to Earth and Fire magic; 25 percent resistance to Chaos and Order magic. Note that the Vampire gains Hit Points for the damage he inflicts.

MISCELLANEOUS UNITS

BAT (DEATH SCOUT)

Str	Dex	Wis	H.P.	Att	Def	Hit Rec	Dam Rec
2	10	5	3	3	4	16	10

Movement: 20

Sight: 5

Stealth: 1

Cost: 4 Ale, 4 Crystals, 13 Gold

Maintenance: 1 Gold

Hit Point Recovery: 1/1/0

DEATH GALLEY (DEATH SHIP)

Str	Dex	Wis	H.P.	Att	Def	Hit Rec	Dam Rec	Missile
0	0	0	30	13	8	30	8	13

Missile Range: 14

Movement: 24

Sight: 5

Stealth: 12

Cost: 19 Ale, 19 Crystals, 56 Gold

Maintenance: 1 Ale, 1 Gold

Hit Point Recovery: 1/1/0

EARTII UNITS

CHAMPIONS AND LORDS

DWARVEN WARLORD (EARTH WARRIOR LORD)

	Exp	Str	Dex	Wis	H.P.	Att	Def	Hit Rec	Dam Rec
Level 1	0	12	8	6	20	14	6	15	2
Level 2	237	12	8	6	23	15	7	15	2
Level 3	548	13	9	6	26	17	9	14	1
Level 4	1,073	14	9	7	29	18	10	13	1
Level 5	1,852	15	10	7	33	20	12	12	0
Level 6	3,032	16	10	7	37	21	13	12	0
Level 7	4,868	17	10	8	41	23	14	11	0
Level 8	7,606	17	9	8	45	23	14	11	0
Level 9	10,605	17	9	8	49	24	15	11	0
Level 10	14,273	17	9	9	52	24	16	11	0
Level 11	18,750	17	8	10	52	25	16	10	0
Level 12	23,525	18	8	11	52	27	17	10	0

Movement: 16

Sight: 3

Stealth: 14

Hit Point Recovery: 4/2/0

MAGICIAN LORD (EARTH MAGE LORD)

	Exp	Str	Dex	Wis	H.P.	Att	Def	Hit Rec	Dam Rec	Mana
Level 1	0	4	8	8	10	2	4	20	2	5
Level 2	262	4	8	9	12	2	4	20	2	6
Level 3	591	5	9	10	13	2	5	20	2	7
Level 4	1,005	5	9	11	13	2	6	19	1	8
Level 5	1,490	5	10	13	14	2	7	19	1	10
Level 6	2,164	6	10	14	15	3	8	18	0	11
Level 7	2,922	6	11	15	15	3	8	18	0	12
Level 8	3,743	6	12	17	16	3	10	17	0	14
Level 9	4,883	7	13	19	17	3	11	17	0	16
Level 10	6,186	7	13	21	17	4	11	16	0	18
Level 11	7,614	7	14	23	18	4	11	15	0	20
Level 12	9,171	8	14	25	18	4	12	15	0	22

Movement: 16

Sight: 4

Stealth: 5

Hit Point Recovery: 4/2/0

Burglar Lord (Earth Thief Lord)

	Exp	Str	Dex	Wis	H.P.	Att	Def	Hit Rec	Dam Rec	Missile
Level 1	0	5	12	8	15	2	4	22	1	6
Level 2	125	5	12	8	16	2	4	21	0	7
Level 3	358	6	13	8	18	3	5	20	0	8
Level 4	657	6	13	9	20	3	5	19	0	9
Level 5	1,012	6	14	9	22	4	7	18	0	9
Level 6	1,824	7	14	9	24	4	7	18	0	10
Level 7	2,725	7	15	10	26	5	8	17	0	11
Level 8	3,713	8	16	10	27	5	10	17	0	13
Level 9	5,345	8	16	10	27	6	10	16	0	13
Level 10	7,059	9	17	11	27	7	10	16	0	14
Level 11	10,322	9	17	12	28	8	10	15	0	14
Level 12	13,783	9	17	13	29	8	11	15	0	15

Missile Range: 12

Movement: 16

Sight: 5

Stealth: 1

Hit Point Recovery: 4/2/0

DWARVEN WARRIOR (EARTH WARRIOR CHAMPION)

	Exp	Str	Dex	Wis	H.P.	Att	Def	Hit Rec	Dam Rec
Level 1	0	11	7	5	16	12	6	15	2
Level 2	237	11	7	5	19	13	7	15	2
Level 3	548	12	8	5	22	15	8	14	1
Level 4	1,073	13	8	6	25	16	9	13	1
Level 5	1,852	14	9	6	29	18	11	12	0
Level 6	3,032	15	9	6	33	19	12	12	0
Level 7	4,868	16	9	7	37	21	13	11	0
Level 8	7,606	16	8	7	41	21	13	11	0
Level 9	10,605	16	8	7	45	22	14	11	0
Level 10	14,273	16	8	8	48	22	15	11	0

Movement: 12

Sight: 2

Stealth: 15

Cost: 29 Ale, 10 Gold

Maintenance: 1 Ale

Hit Point Recovery: 4/2/0

MAGICIAN (EARTH MAGE CHAMPION)

	Exp	Str	Dex	Wis	H.P.	Att	Def	Hit Rec	Dam Rec	Mana
Level 1	0	4	8	10	8	2	3	20	2	3
Level 2	262	4	8	11	10	2	3	20	2	4
Level 3	591	5	9	12	11	2	4	20	2	5
Level 4	1,005	5	9	13	11	2	5	19	1	6
Level 5	1,490	5	10	15	12	2	6	19	1	8
Level 6	2,164	6	10	16	13	3	7	18	0	9
Level 7	2,922	6	11	17	13	3	7	18	0	10
Level 8	3,743	6	12	19	14	3	9	17	0	12
Level 9	4,883	7	13	21	15	3	10	17	0	14
Level 10	6,186	7	13	23	15	4	10	16	0	16

Movement: 12

Sight: 3

Stealth: 6

Cost: 8 Ale, 23 Crystals

Maintenance: 1 Crystal

Hit Point Recovery: 4/2/0

BURGLAR (EARTH THIEF CHAMPION)

	Exp	Str	Dex	Wis	H.P.	Att	Def	Hit Rec	Dam Rec	Missile
Level 1	0	4	11	8	12	2	2	22	1	5
Level 2	125	4	11	8	13	2	2	21	0	6
Level 3	358	5	12	8	15	3	3	20	0	7
Level 4	657	5	12	9	17	3	3	19	0	8
Level 5	1,012	5	13	9	19	4	6	18	0	9
Level 6	1,824	6	13	9	21	4	6	18	0	10
Level 7	2,725	6	14	10	23	5	6	17	0	10
Level 8	3,713	7	15	10	24	5	8	17	0	12
Level 9	5,345	7	15	10	24	6	8	16	0	12
Level 10	7,059	8	16	11	24	6	9	16	0	14

Missile Range: 12

Movement: 12

Sight: 4

Stealth: 2

Cost: 6 Crystals, 19 Gold

Maintenance: 1 Gold

Hit Point Recovery: 4/2/0

CONVENTIONAL UNITS

DWARF INFANTRY (EARTH INFANTRY)

	Exp	Str	Dex	Wis	H.P.	Att	Def	Hit Rec	Dam Rec
Level 1	0	10	5	5	15	9	5	15	6
Level 2	396	11	5	5	21	11	7	15	5
Level 3	1,245	12	5	5	25	13	8	14	4
Level 4	2,649	12	5	6	28	14	9	13	3
Level 5	4,785	13	4	6	30	16	10	12	2

Movement: 10

Sight: 1

Stealth: 15

Cost: 45 Ale, 15 Gold

Maintenance: 1 Ale

Hit Point Recovery: 4/4/2

RIDERS (EARTH CAVALRY)

	Exp	Str	Dex	Wis	H.P.	Att	Def	Hit Rec	Dam Rec
Level 1	0	9	9	6	11	8	4	12	7
Level 2	306	10	10	6	14	10	6	12	7
Level 3	954	10	11	6	17	12	7	11	6
Level 4	1,852	11	12	7	19	14	9	10	5
Level 5	3,882	11	13	7	22	15	11	9	5

Movement: 20

Sight: 2

Stealth: 10

Cost: 36 Ale, 12 Gold

Maintenance: 1 Ale

Hit Point Recovery: 3/3/0

AXE THROWERS (EARTH MISSILE TROOPS)

	Exp	Str	Dex	Wis	H.P.	Att	Def	Hit Rec	Dam Rec	Missile
Level 1	0	10	6	5	12	5	4	19	6	6
Level 2	352	11	6	6	16	7	5	17	5	7
Level 3	846	12	6	6	20	9	6	16	4	8
Level 4	1,712	13	6	7	22	11	7	14	3	10
Level 5	3,188	13	5	7	24	12	8	13	3	11

Missile Range: 7

Movement: 10

Sight: 1

Stealth: 15

Cost: 9 Crystals, 26 Gold

Maintenance: 1 Gold

Hit Point Recovery: 3/3/1

SUMMONED UNITS

SHAMBLER

Str	Dex	Wis	H.P.	Att	Def	Hit Rec	Dam Rec
12	4	4	24	16	8	15	0

Movement: 10

Sight: 1

Stealth: 10

Cost: 10 Ale, 29 Crystals

Maintenance: 1 Crystal

Hit Point Recovery: 4/2/0

25 percent resistance to Earth magic.

GOLEM

Str	Dex	Wis	H.P.	Att	Def	Hit Rec	Dam Rec
14	4	0	32	16	11	30	2

Movement: 16

Sight: 1

Stealth: 12

Cost: 22 Ale, 65 Crystals

Maintenance: 3 Crystals

Hit Point Recovery: 4/2/0

50 percent resistance to Earth magic; 25 percent resistance to Death and Order magic.

STONE GIANT

Str	Dex	Wis	H.P.	Att	Def	Hit Rec	Dam Rec	Missile
18	6	6	50	20	12	18	0	8

Missile Range: 8

Movement: 14

Sight: 3

Stealth: 12

Cost: 56 Ale, 168 Crystals

Maintenance: 5 Crystals

Hit Point Recovery: 4/2/0

75 percent resistance to Earth magic; 50 percent resistance to Death and Order magic; 25 percent resistance to Fire and Water magic.

MISCELLANEOUS UNITS

MITE (EARTH SCOUT)

Str	Dex	Wis	H.P.	Att	Def	Hit Rec	Dam Rec
2	8	5	3	3	2	12	12

Movement: 16
Sight: 4
Stealth: 1
Cost: 2 Ale, 2 Crystals, 6 Gold
Maintenance: 1 Gold
Hit Point Recovery: 4/2/0

BARGE (EARTH SHIP)

Str	Dex	Wis	H.P.	Att	Def	Hit Rec	Dam Rec	Missile
0	0	0	40	14	10	40	8	12

Missile Range: 16
Movement: 20
Sight: 4
Stealth: 12
Cost: 27 Ale, 27 Crystals, 82 Gold
Maintenance: 1 Ale, 1 Gold
Hit Point Recovery: 4/2/0

FIRE UNITS

CHAMPIONS AND LORDS

FIRE WARLORD (FIRE WARRIOR LORD)

	Exp	Str	Dex	Wis	H.P.	Att	Def	Hit Rec	Dam Rec
Level 1	0	13	5	4	24	14	5	6	0
Level 2	230	15	5	4	30	17	6	6	0
Level 3	694	16	5	4	36	19	7	5	0
Level 4	1,450	17	6	5	41	21	7	4	0
Level 5	2,770	17	7	5	47	21	8	3	0
Level 6	4,541	18	8	5	51	22	8	3	0
Level 7	6,602	18	9	6	55	23	10	1	0
Level 8	9,435	19	10	6	57	24	11	1	0
Level 9	12,549	19	10	6	60	24	12	1	0
Level 10	15,892	20	11	7	62	25	12	1	0
Level 11	19,636	21	11	8	64	27	12	0	0
Level 12	23,736	22	11	9	64	28	13	0	0

Movement: 22

Sight: 3

Stealth: 11

Hit Point Recovery: 4/2/0

SORCERESS LORD (FIRE MAGE LORD)

	Exp	Str	Dex	Wis	H.P.	Att	Def	Hit Rec	Dam Rec	Mana
Level 1	0	11	6	8	14	10	2	18	6	5
Level 2	310	12	7	9	17	11	2	18	5	6
Level 3	720	12	8	10	20	11	2	18	5	7
Level 4	1,208	13	8	11	22	13	2	17	5	8
Level 5	1,818	13	8	13	22	13	2	17	4	10
Level 6	2,551	14	9	14	24	15	4	16	4	11
Level 7	3,461	14	9	15	24	15	4	16	4	12
Level 8	4,432	15	9	17	26	17	4	15	4	14
Level 9	5,671	15	10	19	26	17	5	15	3	16
Level 10	7,039	16	10	21	26	18	6	14	3	18
Level 11	8,594	16	10	23	26	18	6	14	3	20
Level 12	10,274	17	10	25	26	19	6	13	3	22

Movement: 22

Sight: 4

Stealth: 10

Hit Point Recovery: 4/2/0

DWARF THIEF LORD (FIRE THIEF LORD)

	Exp	Str	Dex	Wis	H.P.	Att	Def	Hit Rec	Dam Rec	Missile
Level 1	0	10	9	6	17	6	5	28	1	7
Level 2	118	11	10	6	19	8	7	28	0	9
Level 3	293	11	10	6	21	9	8	27	0	9
Level 4	614	12	11	7	23	11	9	26	0	10
Level 5	1,300	12	11	7	25	12	10	25	0	10
Level 6	2,266	13	11	7	27	14	11	24	0	11
Level 7	3,584	13	12	8	29	14	12	23	0	12
Level 8	4,999	13	12	8	31	15	12	22	0	13
Level 9	6,662	13	13	8	31	15	13	21	0	15
Level 10	9,489	14	13	9	31	17	14	20	0	16
Level 11	13,099	14	13	10	32	17	14	19	0	16
Level 12	16,877	15	14	11	33	18	14	18	0	16

Missile Range: 10

Movement: 16

Sight: 4

Stealth: 5

Hit Point Recovery: 4/2/0

FIRE WARRIOR (FIRE WARRIOR CHAMPION)

	Exp	Str	Dex	Wis	H.P.	Att	Def	Hit Rec	Dam Rec
Level 1	0	12	4	3	20	13	4	6	0
Level 2	230	14	4	3	26	16	5	6	0
Level 3	694	15	4	3	32	18	6	5	0
Level 4	1,450	16	5	4	37	20	6	4	0
Level 5	2,770	16	6	4	43	20	7	3	0
Level 6	4,541	17	7	4	47	21	7	3	0
Level 7	6,602	17	8	5	51	22	8	1	0
Level 8	9,435	18	9	5	53	23	9	1	0
Level 9	12,549	18	9	5	56	23	10	1	0
Level 10	15,892	19	10	6	58	24	11	1	0

Movement: 18

Sight: 2

Stealth: 12

Cost: 41 Ale, 14 Gold

Maintenance: 1 Ale

Hit Point Recovery: 4/2/0

FIRE SORCERESS (FIRE MAGE CHAMPION)

	Exp	Str	Dex	Wis	H.P.	Att	Def	Hit Rec	Dam Rec	Mana
Level 1	0	11	5	7	12	10	1	18	6	3
Level 2	310	12	6	8	15	11	1	18	5	4
Level 3	720	12	7	9	18	11	1	18	5	5
Level 4	1,208	13	7	10	20	13	1	17	5	6
Level 5	1,818	13	7	12	20	13	1	17	4	8
Level 6	2,551	14	8	13	22	15	2	16	4	9
Level 7	3,461	14	8	14	22	15	2	16	4	10
Level 8	4,432	15	8	16	24	17	2	15	4	12
Level 9	5,671	15	9	18	24	17	3	15	3	14
Level 10	7,039	16	9	20	24	18	4	14	3	16

Movement: 18

Sight: 3

Stealth: 11

Cost: 9 Ale, 27 Crystals

Maintenance: 1 Crystal

Hit Point Recovery: 4/2/0

DWARVEN THIEF (FIRE THIEF CHAMPION)

	Exp	Str	Dex	Wis	H.P.	Att	Def	Hit Rec	Dam Rec	Missile
Level 1	0	9	8	5	14	4	3	28	1	6
Level 2	118	10	9	5	16	6	5	28	0	8
Level 3	293	10	9	5	18	7	6	27	0	8
Level 4	614	11	10	6	20	9	8	26	0	10
Level 5	1,300	11	10	6	22	10	9	25	0	10
Level 6	2,266	12	10	6	24	12	10	24	0	11
Level 7	3,584	12	11	7	26	12	10	23	0	11
Level 8	4,999	12	11	7	28	13	10	22	0	12
Level 9	6,662	12	12	7	28	13	11	21	0	14
Level 10	9,489	13	12	8	28	15	12	20	0	15

Missile Range: 10

Movement: 12

Sight: 3

Stealth: 6

Cost: 6 Crystals, 18 Gold

Maintenance: 1 Gold

Hit Point Recovery: 4/2/0

CONVENTIONAL UNITS

FLAME BERSERKERS (FIRE INFANTRY)

	Exp	Str	Dex	Wis	H.P.	Att	Def	Hit Rec	Dam Rec
Level 1	0	10	8	4	16	10	2	12	6
Level 2	368	11	9	4	24	13	3	11	6
Level 3	1,278	12	9	4	28	14	3	10	5
Level 4	2,743	13	10	5	32	15	5	10	4
Level 5	4,772	14	11	5	32	17	5	10	3

Movement: 10
Sight: 1
Stealth: 7
Cost: 48 Ale, 16 Gold
Maintenance: 1 Ale
Hit Point Recovery: 4/4/0

FLAME RAIDERS (FIRE CAVALRY)

	Exp	Str	Dex	Wis	H.P.	Att	Def	Hit Rec	Dam Rec
Level 1	0	10	8	4	14	11	2	15	6
Level 2	407	12	8	4	19	15	2	13	6
Level 3	1,377	13	9	4	24	16	3	12	5
Level 4	2,898	14	10	5	26	17	5	11	4
Level 5	4,741	14	10	5	28	18	5	10	3

Movement: 16
Sight: 1
Stealth: 11
Cost: 51 Ale, 17 Gold
Maintenance: 1 Ale
Hit Point Recovery: 3/3/1

ROCKHURLERS (FIRE MISSILE TROOPS)

	Exp	Str	Dex	Wis	H.P.	Att	Def	Hit Rec	Dam Rec	Missile
Level 1	0	11	5	4	16	9	3	13	6	6
Level 2	206	12	5	5	22	11	3	12	4	7
Level 3	530	13	6	5	26	13	4	11	3	8
Level 4	1,014	13	7	6	29	14	4	10	3	10
Level 5	1,931	14	8	6	32	15	5	9	3	11

Missile Range: 10

Movement: 18

Sight: 2

Stealth: 10

Cost: 6 Crystals, 19 Gold

Maintenance: 1 Gold

Hit Point Recovery: 4/2/0

SUMMONED UNITS

FIRE ELEMENTAL

Str	Dex	Wis	H.P.	Att	Def	Hit Rec	Dam Rec
11	8	8	18	20	9	12	4

Movement: 16

Sight: 2

Stealth: 6

Cost: 22 Ale, 66 Crystals

Maintenance: 3 Crystals

Hit Point Recovery: 4/2/0

50 percent resistance to Fire magic; 25 percent resistance to Chaos and Death magic.

DEMON

Str	Dex	Wis	H.P.	Att	Def	Hit Rec	Dam Rec	Missile
17	6	10	46	21	12	13	2	10

Missile Range: 4

Movement: 20

Sight: 4

Stealth: 10

Cost: 57 Ale, 172 Crystals

Maintenance: 5 Crystals

Hit Point Recovery: 4/2/0

75 percent resistance to Fire magic; 50 percent resistance to Chaos and Death magic; 25 percent resistance to Air and Earth magic.

DRAGON

Str	Dex	Wis	H.P.	Att	Def	Hit Rec	Dam Rec	Missile
20	8	12	45	23	12	16	2	18

Missile Range: 8

Movement: 20

Sight: 3

Stealth: 12

Cost: 86 Ale, 257 Crystals

Maintenance: 8 Crystals

Hit Point Recovery: 4/2/0

100 percent resistance to Fire magic; 75 percent resistance to Chaos and Death magic; 50 percent resistance to Air and Earth Magic; 25 percent resistance to Life and Order magic.

MISCELLANEOUS UNITS

IMP (FIRE SCOUT)

Str	Dex	Wis	H.P.	Att	Def	Hit Rec	Dam Rec
4	12	7	6	5	5	12	10

Movement: 20
Sight: 4
Stealth: 2
Cost: 2 Ale, 2 Crystals, 7 Gold
Maintenance: 1 Gold
Hit Point Recovery: 4/2/0

FERRY (FIRE SHIP)

Str	Dex	Wis	H.P.	Att	Def	Hit Rec	Dam Rec	Missile
0	0	0	25	8	4	40	10	8

Missile Range: 8
Movement: 20
Sight: 4
Stealth: 12
Cost: 15 Ale, 15 Crystals, 45 Gold
Maintenance: 1 Ale, 1 Gold
Hit Point Recovery: 4/2/0

LIFE UNITS

CHAMPIONS AND LORDS

ELVEN WARLORD (LIFE WARRIOR LORD)

	Exp	Str	Dex	Wis	H.P.	Att	Def	Hit Rec	Dam Rec
Level 1	0	9	10	7	14	7	6	10	2
Level 2	106	9	11	7	17	8	6	10	2
Level 3	226	10	12	7	20	10	8	9	1
Level 4	478	10	13	8	23	11	9	9	1
Level 5	844	11	13	8	25	13	10	9	1
Level 6	1,388	11	14	8	27	14	10	8	1
Level 7	2,041	12	14	9	29	16	11	8	0
Level 8	2,913	12	15	9	31	17	12	8	0
Level 9	4,191	13	15	9	32	18	13	8	0
Level 10	5,784	13	16	10	33	19	14	8	0
Level 11	7,946	13	17	11	34	20	15	7	0
Level 12	10,735	14	18	12	34	21	17	7	0

Movement: 24

Sight: 4

Stealth: 5

Hit Point Recovery: 3/3/1

ENCHANTRESS LORD (LIFE MAGE LORD)

	Exp	Str	Dex	Wis	H.P.	Att	Def	Hit Rec	Dam Rec	Mana
Level 1	0	4	10	10	10	2	3	20	2	7
Level 2	508	4	11	11	12	2	3	19	2	9
Level 3	1,185	4	12	12	14	2	4	18	2	11
Level 4	2,036	4	13	13	16	3	6	17	2	13
Level 5	3,088	5	14	14	18	3	6	16	1	15
Level 6	4,309	5	14	15	20	3	6	16	1	17
Level 7	5,700	5	15	16	22	4	8	16	1	19
Level 8	7,339	5	15	17	25	4	8	15	0	21
Level 9	9,148	6	16	18	25	4	9	15	0	24
Level 10	11,297	6	16	19	28	5	10	15	0	27
Level 11	13,806	7	17	20	31	6	10	15	0	30
Level 12	16,575	7	18	20	34	6	11	15	0	33

Movement: 18

Sight: 5

Stealth: 3

Hit Point Recovery: 3/3/1

ELVEN THIEF LORD (LIFE THIEF LORD)

	Exp	Str	Dex	Wis	H.P.	Att	Def	Hit Rec	Dam Rec	Missile
Level 1	0	7	13	8	11	4	6	16	1	8
Level 2	219	7	14	8	11	4	6	15	1	9
Level 3	800	7	15	8	12	5	7	14	1	10
Level 4	1,485	8	16	9	13	5	9	14	0	12
Level 5	2,759	8	17	9	14	6	9	13	0	12
Level 6	4,392	8	17	9	15	6	9	13	0	13
Level 7	6,559	9	18	10	16	8	11	12	0	14
Level 8	9,068	9	18	10	17	8	11	12	0	15
Level 9	12,689	10	19	10	18	10	12	11	0	16
Level 10	16,885	10	19	11	19	10	13	11	0	17
Level 11	22,930	11	20	12	20	12	13	10	0	17
Level 12	30,265	11	21	13	21	13	15	10	0	19

Missile Range: 14

Movement: 20

Sight: 7

Stealth: 2

Hit Point Recovery: 3/3/1

ELVEN WARRIOR (LIFE WARRIOR CHAMPION)

	Exp	Str	Dex	Wis	H.P.	Att	Def	Hit Rec	Dam Rec
Level 1	0	8	10	7	10	6	5	10	2
Level 2	106	8	11	7	13	7	5	10	2
Level 3	226	9	12	7	16	9	7	9	1
Level 4	478	9	13	8	19	10	8	9	1
Level 5	844	10	13	8	21	12	9	9	1
Level 6	1,388	10	14	8	23	13	9	8	1
Level 7	2,041	11	14	9	25	15	10	8	0
Level 8	2,913	11	15	9	27	16	11	8	0
Level 9	4,191	12	15	9	28	17	12	8	0
Level 10	5,784	12	16	10	29	18	13	8	0

Movement: 20

Sight: 3

Stealth: 6

Cost: 16 Ale, 5 Gold

Maintenance: 1 Ale

Hit Point Recovery: 3/3/1

ENCHANTRESS (LIFE MAGE CHAMPION)

	Exp	Str	Dex	Wis	H.P.	Att	Def	Hit Rec	Dam Rec	Mana
Level 1	0	4	10	10	8	2	2	20	2	5
Level 2	508	4	11	11	10	2	2	19	2	7
Level 3	1,185	4	12	12	12	2	3	18	2	9
Level 4	2,036	4	13	13	14	3	5	17	2	11
Level 5	3,088	5	14	14	16	3	5	16	1	13
Level 6	4,309	5	14	15	18	3	5	16	1	15
Level 7	5,700	5	15	16	20	4	7	16	1	17
Level 8	7,339	5	15	17	23	4	7	15	0	19
Level 9	9,148	6	16	18	23	4	8	15	0	22
Level 10	11,297	6	16	19	26	5	9	15	0	25

Movement: 14

Sight: 4

Stealth: 4

Cost: 15 Ale, 44 Crystals

Maintenance: 1 Crystal

Hit Point Recovery: 3/3/1

ELVEN THIEF (LIFE THIEF CHAMPION)

	Exp	Str	Dex	Wis	H.P.	Att	Def	Hit Rec	Dam Rec	Missile
Level 1	0	6	12	8	8	4	4	16	1	7
Level 2	219	6	13	8	8	4	5	15	1	9
Level 3	800	6	14	8	9	5	5	14	1	9
Level 4	1,485	7	15	9	10	5	7	14	0	11
Level 5	2,759	7	16	9	11	6	8	13	0	12
Level 6	4,392	7	16	9	12	6	8	13	0	13
Level 7	6,559	8	17	10	13	7	9	12	0	13
Level 8	9,068	8	17	10	14	7	9	12	0	14
Level 9	12,689	9	18	10	15	9	10	11	0	15
Level 10	16,885	9	18	11	16	9	11	11	0	16

Missile Range: 14

Movement: 16

Sight: 6

Stealth: 3

Cost: 14 Crystals, 42 Gold

Maintenance: 1 Gold

Hit Point Recovery: 3/3/1

CONVENTIONAL UNITS

ELVEN STAFFMEN (LIFE INFANTRY)

	Exp	Str	Dex	Wis	H.P.	Att	Def	Hit Rec	Dam Rec
Level 1	0	7	9	6	10	5	3	10	8
Level 2	170	8	10	6	13	6	5	10	8
Level 3	496	8	11	6	15	7	6	9	7
Level 4	1,044	9	12	7	17	9	8	9	7
Level 5	2,046	9	13	7	20	10	10	8	6

Movement: 14

Sight: 3

Stealth: 4

Cost: 19 Ale, 6 Gold

Maintenance: 1 Ale

Hit Point Recovery: 4/4/2

ELVEN RIDERS (LIFE CAVALRY)

	Exp	Str	Dex	Wis	H.P.	Att	Def	Hit Rec	Dam Rec
Level 1	0	7	9	6	9	6	3	10	8
Level 2	223	7	10	6	12	7	5	10	8
Level 3	569	8	11	6	14	9	6	9	7
Level 4	1,251	9	12	7	16	11	8	9	7
Level 5	2,433	9	13	7	18	12	10	8	6

Movement: 22

Sight: 3

Stealth: 10

Cost: 21 Ale, 7 Gold

Maintenance: 1 Ale

Hit Point Recovery: 4/4/1

ELVEN ARCHERS (LIFE MISSILE TROOPS)

	Exp	Str	Dex	Wis	H.P.	Att	Def	Hit Rec	Dam Rec	Missile
Level 1	0	6	10	6	7	1	3	24	10	7
Level 2	343	6	11	7	9	1	3	21	9	9
Level 3	1,097	7	12	7	11	2	5	19	9	11
Level 4	2,555	7	13	8	13	3	6	17	8	13
Level 5	5,085	8	14	8	14	4	6	14	8	14

Missile Range: 16
Movement: 16
Sight: 3
Stealth: 4
Cost: 14 Crystals, 41 Gold
Maintenance: 1 Gold
Hit Point Recovery: 3/5/1

SUMMONED UNITS

DRYAD

Str	Dex	Wis	H.P.	Att	Def	Hit Rec	Dam Rec	Missile
6	12	10	14	3	6	30	10	10

Missile Range: 15
Movement: 14
Sight: 3
Stealth: 4
Cost: 8 Ale, 23 Crystals
Maintenance: 1 Crystal
Hit Point Recovery: 3/3/1

25 percent resistance to Life magic.

UNICORN

Str	Dex	Wis	H.P.	Att	Def	Hit Rec	Dam Rec
14	12	10	35	15	8	10	8

Movement: 24

Sight: 5

Stealth: 5

Cost: 23 Ale, 69 Crystals

Maintenance: 3 Crystals

Hit Point Recovery: 3/3/1

50 percent resistance to Life magic; 25 percent resistance to Air and Water magic.

PEGASUS

Str	Dex	Wis	H.P.	Att	Def	Hit Rec	Dam Rec
14	18	10	31	19	14	11	6

Movement: 24

Sight: 5

Stealth: 10

Cost: 59 Ale, 177 Crystals

Maintenance: 5 Crystals

Hit Point Recovery: 3/3/1

75 percent resistance to Life magic; 50 percent resistance to Air and Water magic; 25 percent resistance to Chaos and Order magic. Note that if the Pegasus survives combat, it automatically heals all damage.

MISCELLANEOUS UNITS

BROWNIE (LIFE SCOUT)

Str	Dex	Wis	H.P.	Att	Def	Hit Rec	Dam Rec
3	12	7	5	4	5	14	10

Movement: 24

Sight: 4

Stealth: 1

Cost: 2 Ale, 2 Crystals, 7 Gold

Maintenance: 1 Gold

Hit Point Recovery: 3/3/1

LIGHT GALLEY (LIFE SHIP)

Str	Dex	Wis	H.P.	Att	Def	Hit Rec	Dam Rec	Missile
0	0	0	25	10	6	25	8	14

Missile Range: 16

Movement: 28

Sight: 5

Stealth: 12

Cost: 24 Ale, 24 Crystals, 73 Gold

Maintenance: 1 Ale, 1 Gold

Hit Point Recovery: 3/3/1

ORDER UNITS

CHAMPIONS AND LORDS

PALADIN LORD (ORDER WARRIOR LORD)

	Exp	Str	Dex	Wis	H.P.	Att	Def	Hit Rec	Dam Rec
Level 1	0	11	8	6	18	13	7	14	1
Level 2	249	11	8	6	22	14	8	14	1
Level 3	610	12	9	6	26	16	10	13	0
Level 4	1,242	13	9	7	30	18	11	13	0
Level 5	2,067	14	10	7	34	20	13	13	0
Level 6	3,509	15	10	7	36	22	14	13	0
Level 7	5,793	15	9	8	40	23	14	12	0
Level 8	8,406	15	10	8	42	23	15	12	0
Level 9	11,252	15	11	8	44	23	15	12	0
Level 10	14,842	15	11	9	46	23	15	11	0
Level 11	18,626	16	11	10	46	25	16	11	0
Level 12	22,902	17	11	11	46	26	17	10	0

Movement: 20

Sight: 3

Stealth: 11

Hit Point Recovery: 4/2/0

WIZARD LORD (ORDER MAGE LORD)

	Exp	Str	Dex	Wis	H.P.	Att	Def	Hit Rec	Dam Rec	Mana
Level 1	0	6	8	8	10	2	1	18	0	5
Level 2	266	6	9	9	11	2	2	18	0	6
Level 3	607	6	10	10	12	2	3	18	0	7
Level 4	1,021	7	10	11	13	2	3	17	0	8
Level 5	1,506	7	11	13	14	3	3	17	0	10
Level 6	2,130	8	11	14	14	3	3	16	0	11
Level 7	2,823	8	12	15	15	3	5	16	0	12
Level 8	3,613	9	12	17	15	5	5	15	0	14
Level 9	4,542	9	13	19	16	5	6	15	0	16
Level 10	5,618	9	13	21	16	5	6	14	0	18
Level 11	6,830	9	14	23	17	5	6	14	0	20
Level 12	8,181	9	14	25	18	6	6	14	0	22

Movement: 16

Sight: 4

Stealth: 7

Hit Point Recovery: 4/2/0

RANGER LORD (ORDER THIEF LORD)

	Exp	Str	Dex	Wis	H.P.	Att	Def	Hit Rec	Dam Rec	Missile
Level 1	0	8	10	6	13	7	6	22	1	8
Level 2	140	8	11	6	15	7	6	20	1	9
Level 3	397	9	12	6	16	9	8	18	1	11
Level 4	857	9	12	7	17	9	8	17	0	12
Level 5	1,536	10	13	7	18	11	10	16	0	13
Level 6	2,514	10	13	7	19	11	10	15	0	14
Level 7	3,784	11	14	8	20	13	11	14	0	14
Level 8	5,897	11	14	8	21	13	11	13	0	15
Level 9	8,227	12	15	8	22	15	13	12	0	16
Level 10	11,144	12	15	9	23	15	13	11	0	17
Level 11	14,898	12	16	10	24	16	15	10	0	18
Level 12	20,534	12	16	11	25	17	15	10	0	18

Missile Range: 10

Movement: 18

Sight: 5

Stealth: 4

Hit Point Recovery: 4/2/0

PALADIN (ORDER WARRIOR CHAMPION)

	Exp	Str	Dex	Wis	H.P.	Att	Def	Hit Rec	Dam Rec
Level 1	0	10	7	6	14	11	7	14	1
Level 2	249	10	7	6	18	12	8	14	1
Level 3	610	11	8	6	22	14	9	13	0
Level 4	1,242	12	8	7	26	16	10	13	0
Level 5	2,067	13	9	7	30	18	12	13	0
Level 6	3,509	14	9	7	32	20	13	13	0
Level 7	5,793	14	8	8	36	21	13	12	0
Level 8	8,406	14	9	8	38	21	14	12	0
Level 9	11,252	14	10	8	40	21	15	12	0
Level 10	14,842	14	10	9	42	21	15	11	0

Movement: 16

Sight: 2

Stealth: 12

Cost: 34 Ale, 11 Gold

Maintenance: 1 Ale

Hit Point Recovery: 4/2/0

WIZARD (ORDER MAGE CHAMPION)

	Exp	Str	Dex	Wis	H.P.	Att	Def	Hit Rec	Dam Rec	Mana
Level 1	0	6	8	8	8	2	0	18	0	3
Level 2	266	6	9	9	9	2	1	18	0	4
Level 3	607	6	10	10	10	2	2	18	0	5
Level 4	1,021	7	10	11	11	2	2	17	0	6
Level 5	1,506	7	11	13	12	3	2	17	0	8
Level 6	2,130	8	11	14	12	3	2	16	0	9
Level 7	2,823	8	12	15	13	3	4	16	0	10
Level 8	3,613	9	12	17	13	5	4	15	0	12
Level 9	4,542	9	13	19	14	5	5	15	0	14
Level 10	5,618	9	13	21	14	5	5	14	0	16

Movement: 12

Sight: 3

Stealth: 8

Cost: 8 Ale, 23 Crystals

Maintenance: 1 Crystal

Hit Point Recovery: 4/2/0

RANGER (ORDER THIEF CHAMPION)

	Exp	Str	Dex	Wis	H.P.	Att	Def	Hit Rec	Dam Rec	Missile
Level 1	0	8	9	6	10	3	4	22	1	7
Level 2	140	8	10	6	12	3	5	20	1	9
Level 3	397	9	11	6	13	5	6	18	1	10
Level 4	857	9	11	7	14	5	6	17	0	11
Level 5	1,536	10	12	7	15	7	8	16	0	12
Level 6	2,514	10	12	7	16	7	8	15	0	13
Level 7	3,784	11	13	8	17	9	10	14	0	14
Level 8	5,897	11	13	8	18	9	10	13	0	15
Level 9	8,227	12	14	8	19	11	11	12	0	15
Level 10	11,144	12	14	9	20	11	11	11	0	16

Missile Range: 10

Movement: 7

Sight: 4

Stealth: 5

Cost: 9 Crystals, 27 Gold

Maintenance: 1 Gold

Hit Point Recovery: 4/2/0

CONVENTIONAL UNITS

FOOTMEN (ORDER INFANTRY)

	Exp	Str	Dex	Wis	H.P.	Att	Def	Hit Rec	Dam Rec
Level 1	0	9	7	6	13	8	5	10	8
Level 2	321	10	8	6	17	10	6	10	7
Level 3	971	11	7	6	20	12	7	9	7
Level 4	1,909	12	6	7	23	14	8	8	6
Level 5	3,719	12	5	7	26	14	9	8	6

Movement: 12
Sight: 1
Stealth: 10
Cost: 35 Ale, 12 Gold
Maintenance: 1 Ale
Hit Point Recovery: 4/4/1

KNIGHTS (ORDER CAVALRY)

	Exp	Str	Dex	Wis	H.P.	Att	Def	Hit Rec	Dam Rec
Level 1	0	9	7	6	12	9	6	18	8
Level 2	533	10	8	6	15	11	8	17	8
Level 3	1,506	11	7	6	18	13	10	15	7
Level 4	3,091	11	6	7	21	14	11	14	6
Level 5	5,671	12	5	7	24	16	12	12	6

Movement: 14
Sight: 1
Stealth: 12
Cost: 51 Ale, 17 Gold
Maintenance: 1 Ale
Hit Point Recovery: 3/2/1

CROSSBOWMEN (ORDER MISSILE TROOPS)

	Exp	Str	Dex	Wis	H.P.	Att	Def	Hit Rec	Dam Rec	Missile
Level 1	0	8	8	6	10	2	4	34	8	8
Level 2	329	8	9	7	13	2	5	31	7	11
Level 3	1,149	9	10	7	15	4	7	28	7	13
Level 4	2,633	10	10	8	17	5	7	25	6	14
Level 5	4,903	10	11	8	20	6	8	22	6	15

Missile Range: 10
Movement: 12
Sight: 2
Stealth: 10
Cost: 15 Crystals, 44 Gold
Maintenance: 1 Gold
Hit Point Recovery: 3/2/1

SUMMONED UNITS

WHITE STAG

Str	Dex	Wis	H.P.	Att	Def	Hit Rec	Dam Rec
12	14	6	20	12	9	12	8

Movement: 24
Sight: 4
Stealth: 4
Cost: 11 Ale, 33 Crystals
Maintenance: 1 Crystal
Hit Point Recovery: 4/2/0

25 percent resistance to Order magic.

GARGOYLE

Str	Dex	Wis	H.P.	Att	Def	Hit Rec	Dam Rec
12	6	6	33	11	11	14	3

Movement: 16

Sight: 2

Stealth: 6

Cost: 2 Ale, 65 Crystals

Maintenance: 3 Crystals

Hit Point Recovery: 4/2/0

50 percent resistance to Order magic; 25 percent resistance to Earth and Water magic.

WARRIOR SPIRIT

Str	Dex	Wis	H.P.	Att	Def	Hit Rec	Dam Rec	Missile
15	8	10	38	18	12	15	4	14

Missile Range: 9

Movement: 16

Sight: 2

Stealth: 12

Cost: 56 Ale, 169 Crystals

Maintenance: 5 Crystals

Hit Point Recovery: 4/2/0

75 percent resistance to Order magic; 50 percent resistance to Earth and Water magic; 25 percent resistance to Death and Life magic.

MISCELLANEOUS UNITS

HOUND (ORDER SCOUT)

Str	Dex	Wis	H.P.	Att	Def	Hit Rec	Dam Rec
6	8	5	8	6	1	12	8

Movement: 20
Sight: 4
Stealth: 4
Cost: 2 Ale, 2 Crystals, 7 Gold
Maintenance: 1 Gold
Hit Point Recovery: 4/2/0

WARSHIP (ORDER SHIP)

Str	Dex	Wis	H.P.	Att	Def	Hit Rec	Dam Rec	Missile
0	0	0	40	14	10	30	6	14

Missile Range: 16
Movement: 24
Sight: 5
Stealth: 12
Cost: 38 Ale, 38 Crystals, 115 Gold
Maintenance: 1 Ale, 1 Gold
Hit Point Recovery: 4/2/0

WATER UNITS

CHAMPIONS AND LORDS

AMAZON WARLORD (WATER WARRIOR LORD)

	Exp	Str	Dex	Wis	H.P.	Att	Def	Hit Rec	Dam Rec
Level 1	0	11	8	6	18	9	5	14	1
Level 2	114	11	9	6	23	10	6	14	1
Level 3	299	12	10	6	28	12	8	13	0
Level 4	676	12	10	7	31	13	8	13	0
Level 5	1,101	13	11	7	34	15	9	13	0
Level 6	1,752	13	12	7	36	16	10	12	0
Level 7	2,772	14	12	8	38	18	11	12	0
Level 8	4,100	14	13	8	40	19	12	12	0
Level 9	5,814	15	13	8	42	20	13	12	0
Level 10	7,947	15	13	9	46	20	13	12	0
Level 11	10,340	16	14	10	46	22	14	12	0
Level 12	13,599	16	14	11	46	22	14	11	0

Movement: 22

Sight: 3

Stealth: 6

Hit Point Recovery: 4/2/0

PRIESTESS LORD (WATER MAGE LORD)

	Exp	Str	Dex	Wis	H.P.	Att	Def	Hit Rec	Dam Rec	Mana
Level 1	0	6	8	9	12	2	1	18	0	6
Level 2	324	6	9	10	14	2	2	17	0	7
Level 3	724	6	9	11	16	3	2	16	0	8
Level 4	1,196	7	10	13	17	4	3	16	0	10
Level 5	1,807	7	11	15	17	5	4	15	0	12
Level 6	2,552	8	11	17	18	5	4	15	0	14
Level 7	3,430	8	12	19	18	5	5	15	0	16
Level 8	4,457	9	12	21	19	7	6	14	0	18
Level 9	5,637	9	13	23	19	7	7	14	0	20
Level 10	7,007	10	13	25	20	8	7	14	0	22
Level 11	8,515	10	14	27	21	8	7	14	0	24
Level 12	10,160	11	14	29	22	9	7	13	0	26

Movement: 18

Sight: 4

Stealth: 6

Hit Point Recovery: 4/2/0

AMAZON THIEF LORD (WATER THIEF LORD)

	Exp	Str	Dex	Wis	H.P.	Att	Def	Hit Rec	Dam Rec	Missile
Level 1	0	8	11	6	15	3	4	15	1	7
Level 2	162	9	12	6	18	6	5	14	0	10
Level 3	581	9	13	6	21	7	6	13	0	13
Level 4	1,535	9	14	7	23	8	6	12	0	13
Level 5	3,059	9	15	7	24	8	8	12	0	14
Level 6	4,766	10	15	7	26	9	8	11	0	15
Level 7	7,635	10	16	8	27	10	9	11	0	16
Level 8	10,794	11	16	8	27	11	10	11	0	16
Level 9	14,229	11	16	8	27	11	10	10	0	17
Level 10	19,199	12	17	9	27	13	11	10	0	17
Level 11	24,846	12	17	10	28	13	11	10	0	17
Level 12	30,556	12	17	11	29	14	12	10	0	18

Missile Range: 9

Movement: 18

Sight: 5

Stealth: 3

Hit Point Recovery: 4/2/0

AMAZON WARRIOR (WATER WARRIOR CHAMPION)

	Exp	Str	Dex	Wis	H.P.	Att	Def	Hit Rec	Dam Rec
Level 1	0	10	8	6	14	8	4	14	1
Level 2	114	10	9	6	19	9	5	14	1
Level 3	299	11	10	6	24	11	7	13	0
Level 4	676	11	10	7	27	12	7	13	0
Level 5	1,101	12	11	7	30	14	8	13	0
Level 6	1,752	12	12	7	32	15	9	12	0
Level 7	2,772	13	12	8	34	17	10	12	0
Level 8	4,100	13	13	8	36	18	11	12	0
Level 9	5,814	14	13	8	38	19	12	12	0
Level 10	7,947	14	13	9	42	19	12	12	0

Movement: 18

Sight: 2

Stealth: 7

Cost: 21 Ale, 7 Gold

Maintenance: 1 Ale

Hit Point Recovery: 4/2/0

PRIESTESS (WATER MAGE CHAMPION)

	Exp	Str	Dex	Wis	H.P.	Att	Def	Hit Rec	Dam Rec	Mana
Level 1	0	6	8	10	10	2	0	18	1	6
Level 2	324	6	9	11	12	2	1	17	0	7
Level 3	724	6	9	12	14	3	1	16	0	8
Level 4	1,196	7	10	14	15	4	2	16	0	10
Level 5	1,807	7	11	16	15	5	3	15	0	12
Level 6	2,552	8	11	18	16	5	3	15	0	14
Level 7	3,430	8	12	20	16	5	4	15	0	16
Level 8	4,457	9	12	22	17	7	5	14	0	18
Level 9	5,637	9	13	24	17	7	6	14	0	20
Level 10	7,007	10	13	26	18	8	6	14	0	22

Movement: 12

Sight: 3

Stealth: 7

Cost: 9 Ale, 26 Crystals

Maintenance: 1 Crystal

Hit Point Recovery: 4/2/0

AMAZON THIEF (WATER THIEF CHAMPION)

	Exp	Str	Dex	Wis	H.P.	Att	Def	Hit Rec	Dam Rec	Missile
Level 1	0	8	10	6	12	3	3	15	2	7
Level 2	162	9	11	6	15	6	3	14	1	9
Level 3	581	9	12	6	18	7	4	13	1	12
Level 4	1,535	9	13	7	20	8	5	12	1	13
Level 5	3,059	9	14	7	21	8	6	12	0	13
Level 6	4,766	10	14	7	23	9	6	11	0	14
Level 7	7,635	10	15	8	24	10	7	11	0	15
Level 8	10,794	11	15	8	24	11	8	11	0	15
Level 9	14,229	11	15	8	24	11	8	10	0	16
Level 10	19,199	12	16	9	24	13	10	10	0	17

Missile Range: 9

Movement: 14

Sight: 4

Stealth: 4

Cost: 17 Crystals, 52 Gold

Maintenance: 1 Gold

Hit Point Recovery: 4/2/0

CONVENTIONAL UNITS

LIZARDMEN (WATER INFANTRY)

	Exp	Str	Dex	Wis	H.P.	Att	Def	Hit Rec	Dam Rec
Level 1	0	9	8	2	14	7	3	12	8
Level 2	256	10	8	2	18	9	4	12	7
Level 3	729	11	9	2	21	11	6	11	7
Level 4	1,633	12	10	3	25	12	8	10	6
Level 5	3,050	12	11	3	28	13	8	9	6

Movement: 16
Sight: 2
Stealth: 6
Cost: 26 Ale, 9 Gold
Maintenance: 1 Ale
Hit Point Recovery: 4/2/0

HEAVY CAVALRY (WATER CAVALRY)

	Exp	Str	Dex	Wis	H.P.	Att	Def	Hit Rec	Dam Rec
Level 1	0	9	7	6	12	9	6	18	8
Level 2	533	10	8	6	15	11	8	17	8
Level 3	1,506	11	7	6	18	13	10	15	7
Level 4	3,091	11	6	7	21	14	11	14	6
Level 5	5,671	12	5	7	24	16	12	12	6

Movement: 14
Sight: 1
Stealth: 12
Cost: 51 Ale, 17 Gold
Maintenance: 1 Ale
Hit Point Recovery: 3/2/1

SLINGERS (WATER MISSILE TROOPS)

	Exp	Str	Dex	Wis	H.P.	Att	Def	Hit Rec	Dam Rec	Missile
Level 1	0	8	9	2	10	3	4	19	8	5
Level 2	302	8	10	3	14	4	6	17	7	7
Level 3	1,016	9	11	3	16	6	7	16	7	8
Level 4	1,882	10	12	4	18	7	9	14	6	10
Level 5	3,895	11	12	4	20	9	9	13	5	11

Missile Range: 10
Movement: 16
Sight: 2
Stealth: 7
Cost: 13 Crystals, 39 Gold
Maintenance: 1 Gold
Hit Point Recovery: 3/3/1

SUMMONED UNITS

WATER ELEMENTAL

Str	Dex	Wis	H.P.	Att	Def	Hit Rec	Dam Rec
14	10	5	30	15	5	15	2

Movement: 16
Sight: 2
Stealth: 4
Cost: 10 Ale, 30 Crystals
Maintenance: 1 Crystal
Hit Point Recovery: 4/2/0

25 percent resistance to Water magic.

KRAKEN

Str	Dex	Wis	H.P.	Att	Def	Hit Rec	Dam Rec	Missile
16	6	2	39	18	9	13	2	8

Missile Range: 10
Movement: 24
Sight: 3
Stealth: 2
Cost: 21 Ale, 64 Crystals
Maintenance: 3 Crystals
Hit Point Recovery: 4/2/0

50 percent resistance to Water magic; 25 percent resistance to Life and Order magic.

SERPENT

Str	Dex	Wis	H.P.	Att	Def	Hit Rec	Dam Rec	Missile
18	8	6	55	21	12	13	0	10

Missile Range: 6
Movement: 30
Sight: 3
Stealth: 2
Cost: 61 Ale, 184 Crystals
Maintenance: 6 Crystals
Hit Point Recovery: 4/2/0

100 percent resistance to Water magic; 75 percent resistance to Life and Order magic; 50 percent resistance to Air and Earth magic; 25 percent resistance to Chaos and Death magic.

MISCELLANEOUS UNITS

SEAGULL (WATER SCOUT)

Str	Dex	Wis	H.P.	Att	Def	Hit Rec	Dam Rec
2	10	5	4	3	2	14	10

Movement: 24
Sight: 5
Stealth: 3
Cost: 4 Ale, 4 Crystals, 13 Gold
Maintenance: 1 Gold
Hit Point Recovery: 4/2/0

CORSAIR (WATER SHIP)

Str	Dex	Wis	H.P.	Att	Def	Hit Rec	Dam Rec	Missile
0	0	0	30	12	8	25	6	14

Missile Range: 14
Movement: 36
Sight: 6
Stealth: 6
Cost: 27 Ale, 27 Crystals, 81 Gold
Maintenance: 1 Ale, 1 Gold
Hit Point Recovery: 4/2/0

CHAPTER

8

ARTIFACTS

This chapter is a quick reference guide to every artifact in **Lords of Magic**. In addition to artifact names and powers, this chapter has tables that show you which faiths and character classes can use which artifacts. Use this chapter to look up individual artifacts, or read through it to learn what sort of artifacts you can expect to find scattered through the lands of Urak.

GREATER ARTIFACTS

As one might expect, Greater Artifacts tend to have superior powers compared to the benefits of Lesser Artifacts. You always will find Greater Artifacts in dungeons.

Each faith has three Greater Artifacts, one for each class. (Death actually has four, one for each class and one specifically for Balkoth.) Some Greater Artifacts can be wielded by more than one faith, but the faith that the artifact pertains to receives extra benefits when it wields its own artifact. For example, Air or Life Thieves can wield Air's Bow of Quaal; but while Air Thieves can slow a target down with a successful hit, Life Thieves don't get this bonus effect.

Each artifact entry contains the following information:

- Allowed Classes tells you which classes can use a particular artifact.

- Allowed Faiths tells you which faiths can use the artifact.

- Wield Position tells you which hand can wield the artifact: Left, Right, or Either.

> Many artifacts, both Greater and Lesser, can be wielded by members of several faiths, but one particular faith gets more value out of the artifact than the others. Whenever this is the case, the Allowed Faiths column shows the "enhanced value" faith in italics. The other faiths, which can use the artifact but not as effectively, are listed in regular type.
>
> Read the artifact description to learn what extra benefits the "enhanced value" faith enjoys.

AIR ARTIFACTS

BOW OF QUAAL

Allowed Classes: Thief
Allowed Faiths: Air, Life
Wield Position: Right

The Bow of Quaal gives its wielder +2 Dexterity, +2 Ranged Attack, +2 Missile Range, and +1 Attack Recovery. Wielders of the Air faith have a chance at slowing targets on impact.

> Astute readers will note that Attack Recovery is, in fact, better when it's lower. In this chapter, however, whenever we say that an artifact conveys a positive bonus to Attack Recovery, what we really mean is that it subtracts from Attack Recovery's total. We just thought it would be confusing to say that artifacts give a negative "bonus."
>
> The bottom line? Just remember that any artifact that affects Attack Recovery is a good thing.

STAFF OF ASPHYXIATION

Allowed Classes: Mage
Allowed Faiths: All, Air
Wield Position: Right

The Staff of Asphyxiation grants its wielder +6 Mana. Wielders of the Air faith also gain 50 percent resistance to Earth magic and 40 percent resistance to all other magic. The Air faith can also cast Asphyxiate once each day and has a chance to asphyxiate opponents physically struck in combat.

THUNDERBLADE

Allowed Classes: Warrior
Allowed Faiths: Air, Fire
Wield Position: Right

Thunderblade gives its wielder +4 Attack and +2 Defense. Wielders of the Air faith also gain five for Attack Recovery, receive +1 fame daily, and may cast one Thunderclap per day, stunning enemies within a large radius.

CHAOS ARTIFACTS

AMULET OF FATE

Allowed Classes: Thief
Allowed Faiths: All, Chaos
Wield Position: Either

The Amulet of Fate grants its wielder +2 Dexterity, +3 Luck, and the ability to cast Polymorph Self. It also gives +1 gold for each level of the wielder per turn. Also, Chaos Thieves gain 2,000 experience points and receive an additional +2 bonus to Dexterity.

> **Luck is simply a general bonus to combat and Thief-related activities.**

AXE OF CHAOS

Allowed Classes: Warrior
Allowed Faiths: Chaos, Earth
Wield Position: Either

The Axe of Chaos grants its wielder random modifiers (determined at the beginning of each combat) to the following statistics:

Attack: A random number between −2 and +6

Attack Recovery: A random number between −2 and +4

Hit Recovery: A random number between −2 and +4

Wielders from Chaos also receive +3 Luck, +1,500 experience, and a small chance of unleashing Petrify, Polymorph Other, Lightning Bolt, or Curse when striking an opponent in melee.

POLYMORPH STAFF

Allowed Classes: Mage
Allowed Faiths: All, Chaos
Wield Position: Right

The Polymorph Staff gives its wielder +3 Attack, +6 Wisdom, and the ability to cast Polymorph Other. Wielders from Chaos also gain two Defense and have a chance of polymorphing enemies into random units when they are struck in melee.

DEATH ARTIFACTS

BALKOTH'S SCYTHE

> **Unique Artifact for Balkoth alone**

Allowed Classes: Mage
Allowed Faiths: Death
Wield Position: Right

Balkoth's Scythe grants Balkoth +3 crystals per level, +3 Mana, and the ability to cast Locust once per day. In combat, Balkoth is given +3 to Attack and Ranged Attack, +1 Vampiric life stealing, and a chance to claim an opponent's soul—which, by the way, kills the opponent—with each successful hit in combat.

> **"Vampiric life stealing"** simply means that Balkoth takes Hit Points away from an enemy and adds them to his own Hit Point total.

LIFE STEALING BLADE

Allowed Classes: Thief
Allowed Faiths: Death
Wield Position: Right

The Life Stealing Blade grants a Death Thief +2 Attack, +2 Ranged Attack, +1 Missile Range, and +1 Attack Recovery. In addition, there is a small chance that an opponent struck in combat will be paralyzed (similar to Air's Stun spell) and will lose 1,000 in experience.

SOUL STEALER

Allowed Classes: Warrior
Allowed Faiths: Death, Order, Water
Wield Position: Right

Soul Stealer gives its wielder +2 Attack, +2 Attack Recovery, and the ability to cast Curse. If a Death Warrior has this artifact, Soul Stealer gives +1 Defense, an additional +1 Attack, and a small chance that every strike will be a "vorpal" Attack, which kills the opponent and gives the Death Warrior 200 in experience.

STAFF OF ANIMATION

Allowed Classes: Mage
Allowed Faiths: All, Death
Wield Position: Right

The Staff of Animation grants its wielder +1 Defense and the ability to cast the Death spell Raise Shade. The staff also heals its wielder, like Life's spell Cure Wounds, at the start of combat. If a Death Mage wields this artifact, the staff raises its owner's Attack by three and Mana by six.

EARTH ARTIFACTS

AXE OF MAULING

Allowed Classes: Warrior
Allowed Faiths: Chaos, Earth
Wield Position: Right

The Axe of Mauling gives its wielder +2 Attack and the ability to cast Tremor, a special spell that deals damage to all units in combat. When handled by an Earth Warrior, this axe also grants +3 Attack Recovery, +1 fame per day, a 2,000 point experience bonus, and an additional +1 Attack.

BOW OF BALLADRINE

Allowed Classes: Thief
Allowed Faiths: Air, Earth, Life
Wield Position: Right

The Bow of Balladrine grants its wielder +2 Ranged Attack, +1 Missile Range, +1 Attack Recovery, and the ability to cast the Earth spell Rocksling. Earth Thieves also gain an additional one for Ranged Attack and receive +2 Stealth.

GORGON'S STAFF

Allowed Classes: Mage
Allowed Faiths: All, Earth
Wield Position: Right

The Gorgon's Staff grants its wielder +1 Attack, +1 Defense, +3 Wisdom, and the ability to cast Petrify, which turns one victim into stone regardless of his level. This artifact doubles the Attack, Defense, and Wisdom bonuses of an Earth Mage when he holds it. In addition, the Earth Mage may possibly petrify opponents they strike in melee.

FIRE ARTIFACTS

THE SPITFIRE

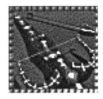

Allowed Classes: Thief
Allowed Faiths: Fire, Order
Wield Position: Right

The Spitfire gives its wielder +2 Ranged Attack, +1 Missile Range, +1 Missile Speed, and the ability to cast the Fire spell Fireball. Fire Thieves also receive +5 Attack Recovery and an additional +1 for Ranged Attack, Missile Range, and Missile Speed.

STAFF OF INCINERATION

Allowed Classes: Mage
Allowed Faiths: All, Fire
Wield Position: Right

The Staff of Incineration grants its wielder +6 Mana and the ability to cast Backdraft, a multiple Fireball spell. A Fire Mage who holds this staff gains 50 percent resistance against Water magic, 25 percent resistance to all other magic, and a +3 bonus for Defense. He also has a chance of Scalding an opponent in melee with a successful hit.

> Scald is a special Fire spell that causes one point of damage to its target every two seconds for ten seconds.
>
> Backdraft is an area-effect spell that deals six points of damage to all units within a radius determined by the caster's level.

SWORD OF FLAMES

Allowed Classes: Warrior
Allowed Faiths: Air, Fire
Wield Position: Right

The Sword of Flames grants its wielder +3 Attack and the ability to cast Flame Dart. In addition, Fire Warriors gain improved combat speeds, receive +3 Luck, and +1 Defense, and they have a chance of burning enemies for extra damage with a successful hit in melee.

LIFE ARTIFACTS

BOW OF BAKAL

Allowed Classes: Thief
Allowed Faiths: Air, Earth, Life
Wield Position: Right

The Bow of Bakal gives its wielder +1 Ranged Attack, +2 Missile Range, +1 Attack Recovery, and the ability to cast the Life spell Spirit Arrow. If a Life Thief holds the bow, he receives an additional +1 Ranged Attack and a 50 percent missile Attack resistance.

STAFF OF LIGHT

Allowed Classes: Warrior, Mage
Allowed Faiths: Life
Wield Position: Right

The Staff of Light grants its wielder +4 Attack, +2 Defense, and the ability to cast the Life spell Ray of Hope. The staff also casts the spell Holy Visit at the beginning of combat, acts as a permanent Regeneration spell in combat, and restores the wielder to full health at the end of combat.

RESURRECTION STAFF

Allowed Classes: Mage
Allowed Faiths: All, Life
Wield Position: Right

The Resurrection Staff gives its wielder +2 Defense, +6 Mana, and the ability to cast Resurrection. When wielded by a Life Mage, the staff also grants 40 percent resistance to Death magic, acts as a permanent Regeneration spell in combat, restores the wielder to full health at the end of combat, and gives the Mage a chance of using a Spirit Arrow to cause extra damage to a unit struck in melee.

ORDER ARTIFACTS

CROSSBOW OF BALANCE

Allowed Classes: Thief
Allowed Faiths: Fire, Order
Wield Position: Right

The Crossbow of Balance grants its wielder +2 Ranged Attack, +1 Missile Range, +2 Attack Recovery, +2 Stealth, and the ability to cast Righteous Bolt. An Order Thief also receives from the Crossbow an additional +1 Ranged Attack, an additional +1 Missile Range, and an additional +3 Attack Recovery.

GUARDIAN

Allowed Classes: Warrior
Allowed Faiths: Death, Order, Water
Wield Position: Right

Guardian gives its wielder +2 Attack, +2 Attack Recovery, and +2 Luck. It also grants +1 fame per turn. When wielded by an Order Warrior, Guardian also casts the Order spell Morale at the beginning of combat, gives its wielder an additional +1 Attack and +1 Luck and has a chance of instantly killing an enemy struck in melee.

RING OF PRODUCTIVITY

Allowed Classes: All
Allowed Faiths: Order
Wield Position: Either

The Ring of Productivity grants its wielder +2 Defense, +6 Mana, 40 percent resistance to all forms of magic, and the ability to reduce—for one turn—enemy cities' production by one for each level of the wielder. In addition, for every turn, one component of the wielder's production gains two for every level of the wielder.

WATER ARTIFACTS

BLOWGUN OF THE AMAZONS

Allowed Classes: Thief
Allowed Faiths: Water
Wield Position: Right

The Blowgun of the Amazons grants its wielder +2 Ranged Attack, +2 Missile Range, +1 Missile Speed, and the ability to cast the Water spell Ice Bolt. In addition, enemies struck by the blowgun may possibly be sealed in a coffin of ice.

ROCCA'S CHALICE

Allowed Classes: All
Allowed Faiths: All, Water (yes, Water, not Chaos)
Wield Position: Either

Rocca's Chalice gives its wielder +2 Wisdom and +1 ale production per wielder level per turn. If a Water Champion holds the chalice, he also receives 500 experience points.

STAFF OF DROWNING

Allowed Classes: Mage
Allowed Faiths: All, Water
Wield Position: Right

The Staff of Drowning grants its wielder +2 Defense, +6 Mana, and the ability to cast Drowning—a special spell that fills all units' lungs within a short radius with water, damaging all non-Water units and healing Water units. This staff also gives Mages of the Water faith +2 Wisdom and a chance of Drowning any units hit in melee.

TIDALBLADE

Allowed Classes: Warrior
Allowed Faiths: Death, Order, Water
Wield Position: Right

Tidalblade gives its wielder +2 Attack, +2 Dexterity, +1 Attack Recovery, and the ability to cast Ice Bolt. For Warriors of the Water faith, Tidalblade also gives +1 fame per turn, bestows an additional +2 Attack Recovery, and has a chance of causing rust when it hits an opponent in melee, consequently inflicting a –1 penalty against the target's Defense.

LESSER ARTIFACTS

Lesser Artifacts can be found in many locations. Although their effects are typically less dramatic than those of Greater Artifacts, they can still be extremely valuable.

AIR ARTIFACTS

ARAMOUG'S AMULET

Allowed Classes: Thief
Allowed Faiths: All, Air
Wield Position: Either

Aramoug's Amulet grants its wielder +2 Defense. Air Thieves also acquire +2 Sight and the ability to cast one Area Stun spell per day, which is essentially a Stun spell capable of affecting enemies within a large radius.

CLOUDSTAFF

Allowed Classes: Mage
Allowed Faiths: All
Wield Position: Right

The Cloudstaff grants its wielder +1 Defense and +2 Mana.

EYES OF THE HAWK

Allowed Classes: Warrior, Mage
Allowed Faiths: Air, Life, Order
Wield Position: Either

The Eyes of the Hawk grants its wielder +3 Mana, +3 Sight Radius, and the ability to cast the Air spell Seer.

FAERIE RING

Allowed Classes: Thief
Allowed Faiths: All
Wield Position: Either

The Faerie Ring grants its wielder +1 Defense and +1 Ranged Attacks.

FEATHER CHAIN MAIL

Allowed Classes: Warrior
Allowed Faiths: Air, Fire
Wield Position: Left

Feather Chain Mail gives it holder +3 Defense and 40 percent resistance against Earth magic. Air Warriors also receive +2 Dexterity, +2 Movement, and 30 percent resistance to all magic (except for Earth magic, which remains at 40 percent).

ICE SWORD

Allowed Classes: Warrior
Allowed Faiths: Death, Order, Water
Wield Position: Right

The Ice Sword grants its wielder +1 Attack and +1 Defense.

KAPELKE'S RING

Allowed Classes: All
Allowed Faiths: Air, Life, Order
Wield Position: Either

Kapelke's Ring grants its wielder +1 Defense, +2 Movement, and the ability to cast Life's Heal spell once daily.

PIXIE DUST

Allowed Classes: Thief
Allowed Faiths: Air, Chaos, Life
Wield Position: Either

Pixie Dust lets its wielder unleash Pixies, reducing the targets' Sight Radius by two and Dexterity by one. In combat, each hit with Pixie Dust reduces the target's Missile Range by one.

RING OF THE FOUR WINDS

Allowed Classes: Mage
Allowed Faiths: All, Air
Wield Position: Either

The Ring of the Four Winds grants its wielder +1 Defense, +3 Mana and 25 percent resistance to all magic. Air Mages also gain 25 percent resistance to missiles and an additional +2 Defense.

STORMBREAKER

Allowed Classes: Warrior
Allowed Faiths: Air, Fire
Wield Position: Right

Stormbreaker gives its wielder +1 Attack and +1 Defense.

CHAOS ARTIFACTS

AMULET OF CHANCE

Allowed Classes: Mage
Allowed Faiths: All
Wield Position: Either

The Amulet of Chance grants its wielder +1 Defense and +2 Mana.

AMULET OF ILLUSION

Allowed Classes: All
Allowed Faiths: Chaos
Wield Position: Either

The Amulet of Illusion grants its wielder +3 Defense, +3 Mana, +2 Movement, and the ability to cast Confusion.

AMULET OF INDECISION

Allowed Classes: All
Allowed Faiths: All, Chaos
Wield Position: Either

The Amulet of Indecision grants its wielder +2 Defense and +1 Luck and adds 10 to the wielder's maximum Hit Points. In combat, a Chaos Champion with this amulet may temporarily freeze an enemy in a coffin of ice, which paralyzes the victim for a full minute.

CHAKRAM OF ENTROPY

Allowed Classes: Thief
Allowed Faiths: Chaos
Wield Position: Right

The Chakram of Entropy gives its owner +3 Ranged Attack, +2 Missile Range, +1 Attack Recovery, and 30 percent resistance to missile attacks. In addition, there is a chance that an enemy struck by the wielder of the Chakram will be randomly teleported to another area of the combat arena.

GREAT AXE

Allowed Classes: Warrior
Allowed Faiths: Chaos, Earth
Wield Position: Right

The Great Axe grants its wielder +1 Defense and +1 Sight Radius.

HELM OF ASYMMETRY

Allowed Classes: Warrior
Allowed Faiths: Chaos, Earth
Wield Position: Either

The Helm of Asymmetry grants its wielder +2 Defense, 30 percent resistance against Order magic, and 25 percent resistance to all other magic. In addition, the helm gives Chaos Warriors two points for Sight Radius and an additional two points for Defense.

RING OF ANYTHING

Allowed Classes: Mage
Allowed Faiths: All
Wield Position: Either

The Ring of Anything grants its wielder an increase in production of a resource, randomly selected each turn; this resource is increased one point for every level of the wielder. In addition, the caster gains the ability to cast one of the following spells (again, selected randomly each turn): Heal, Commune with Nature, Fireball, or Polymorph Self.

RING OF MAZES

Allowed Classes: Thief
Allowed Faiths: All, Chaos
Wield Position: Either

The Ring of Mazes grants its wielder +2 Strength, +2 Movement, and the ability to cast Confusion. Chaos Thieves also receive +2 for their Sight Radius.

RING OF STEALTH

Allowed Classes: Thief
Allowed Faiths: All
Wield Position: Either

The Ring of Stealth grants its wielder +1 for Defense and +1 for Stealth.

DEATH ARTIFACTS

AMULET OF POISON

Allowed Classes: Thief
Allowed Faiths: All, Death
Wield Position: Either

The Amulet of Poison grants its wielder +2 Defense and +2 Stealth. As with Death's Decay spell, Thieves of the Death faith have a chance of poisoning enemies struck in combat.

ASHES OF INFESTATION

Allowed Classes: All
Allowed Faiths: Death
Wield Position: Either

The Ashes of Infestation grants its wielder +1 Attack, +1 Defense, +2 Luck, and the ability to cast Death's Spawn spell.

DARKBLADE

Allowed Classes: Warrior
Allowed Faiths: Death, Order, Water
Wield Position: Right

Darkblade grants its wielder +1 Attack and +1 Movement.

DEATH DAGGER

Allowed Classes: Thief
Allowed Faiths: Death
Wield Position: Right

The Death Dagger grants its wielder +1 Attack and +1 Ranged Attack.

EBONY PLATE OF THE VOID

Allowed Classes: Warrior
Allowed Faiths: Death, Earth, Order
Wield Position: Left

The Ebony Plate of the Void grants its wielder +2 Defense and 20 percent magic resistance. When wielded by a Death Warrior, the plate bestows an additional +1 Defense, increases resistance against Life magic to 30 percent, and gives the wielder a chance of inflicting Decay upon opponents it hits in combat.

LICH CLOAK

Allowed Classes: Mage
Allowed Faiths: Chaos, Death, Earth, Fire
Wield Position: Left

The Lich Cloak grants its wielder +2 Defense; +3 Mana; 40 percent resistance to Life magic; 30 percent resistance to Air, Order, and Water magic; and 20 percent resistance to Chaos, Death, Earth, and Fire magic. A Death Mage killed while wearing the Lich Cloak becomes a Vampire.

RING OF AZZ'TARUTH

Allowed Classes: Mage
Allowed Faiths: All, Death
Wield Position: Either

The Ring of Azz'taruth grants its wielder +1 Defense, +3 Mana, and the ability to cast Decay. When wielded by a Mage of the Death faith, this ring also bestows 20 percent resistance against magic.

RING OF LEECHES

Allowed Classes: All
Allowed Faiths: Death
Wield Position: Either

The Ring of Leeches gives its wielder +1 Defense, +1 Strength, and the ability to cast Leeches, transferring four Hit Points from the target to the ring's wielder.

SHADOWSTAFF

Allowed Classes: Mage
Allowed Faiths: All
Wield Position: Right

The Shadowstaff grants its wielder +1 Defense and +2 Mana.

EARTH ARTIFACTS

CRYSTAL RING

Allowed Classes: Warrior
Allowed Faiths: All, Earth
Wield Position: Either

The Crystal Ring grants its wielder +2 Defense, +2 Damage Recovery, and 25 percent resistance to Air magic. In addition, the Crystal Ring restores its wearer to full Hit Points at the end of combat. When an Earth Warrior wears this ring, it doubles the resistance to Air Magic to 50 percent and gives +1 Attack, too.

CRYSTALMIGHT

Allowed Classes: Mage
Allowed Faiths: Earth
Wield Position: Either

Crystalmight grants its wielder +3 Mana, +1,000 experience points, and +2 crystals per wielder level for every turn.

GOLDENROD

Allowed Classes: Mage
Allowed Faiths: All
Wield Position: Right

Goldenrod grants its wielder +2 Mana and +1 Movement.

LUCKSTONE

Allowed Classes: All
Allowed Faiths: All
Wield Position: Either

The Luckstone grants its wielder +3 Luck, +1 Strength, +1 Dexterity, +1 Sight Radius, +1 Attack Recovery, and a 30 percent resistance against Air magic.

OBSIDIAN PLATE

Allowed Classes: Warrior
Allowed Faiths: Death, Earth, Order
Wield Position: Left

In addition to restoring all Hit Points after combat, Obsidian Plate grants its wielder +2 Defense and +3 gold per turn. An Earth Warrior with this plate also receives an additional +1 for Defense, 50 percent resistance against Air magic, and one Hit Point of damage for every seven seconds in battle.

REED BOW

Allowed Classes: Thief
Allowed Faiths: Air, Earth, Life
Wield Position: Right

The Reed Bow grants its wielder +1 for its Ranged Attack and +1 for its Sight Radius.

RING OF ENTANGLEMENT

Allowed Classes: Thief
Allowed Faiths: All
Wield Position: Either

The Ring of Entanglement grants its wielder +1 Defense, +2 Dexterity, +2 Movement, and the ability to cast the Earth spell Entanglement.

STONE RING

Allowed Classes: Mage
Allowed Faiths: All, Earth
Wield Position: Either

The Stone Ring grants its wielder +2 Defense, 10 percent magic resistance, and the ability to cast the Earth spell Clay Earth. When an Earth Mage wears the Stone Ring, resistance to all magic is doubled to 20 percent, except for resistance against Air magic, which is tripled to 30 percent.

SWIFT AXE

Allowed Classes: Warrior
Allowed Faiths: Chaos, Earth
Wield Position: Right

The Swift Axe gives its wielder +1 Attack and +1 Sight Radius.

Fire Artifacts

Borchert's Torch

Allowed Classes: Thief
Allowed Faiths: All, Fire
Wield Position: Either

Borchert's Torch grants the holder +1 Sight Radius, +2 Movement, and 20 percent resistance to magic. When held by a Fire Thief, the Torch also provides an additional +2 to the Thief's Sight Radius and increases the Missile Range of all friendly units by 25 percent.

Burning Blade

Allowed Classes: Warrior
Allowed Faiths: Air, Fire
Wield Position: Right

The Burning Blade grants its wielder +1 Attack and +1 Defense.

Dragonscale Armor

Allowed Classes: Warrior
Allowed Faiths: Air, Fire
Wield Position: Left

Dragonscale Armor grants its wielder +3 Defense and 50 percent resistance to Water and Fire magic. When a Fire Warrior wears this armor, he has a chance of dealing additional damage with each successful strike on the enemy.

Eternal Flame

Allowed Classes: All
Allowed Faiths: Fire
Wield Position: Either

The Eternal Flame grants its holder +1 Defense and 1,000 experience points.

FLAMESHAFT

Allowed Classes: Mage
Allowed Faiths: All
Wield Position: Right

The Flameshaft grants its wielder +2 Mana and +1 Movement.

FLINT RING

Allowed Classes: Thief
Allowed Faiths: All
Wield Position: Either

The Flint Ring grants its wielder +1 Defense and +1 Attack Recovery.

RING OF BRIMSTONE

Allowed Classes: All
Allowed Faiths: Fire
Wield Position: Either

The Ring of Brimstone heals its wielder of all damage at the end of battle, grants him +2 Movement, and allows him to cast the special spell Fireheal, which restores one Hit Point every two seconds for ten seconds in combat.

RING OF THE DANCING FLAMES

Allowed Classes: All
Allowed Faiths: Fire
Wield Position: Either

The Ring of the Dancing Flames gives its owner +2 Defense, +2 Dexterity, +2 Movement, and +3 gold per turn.

RING OF EMBERS

Allowed Classes: Mage
Allowed Faiths: Chaos, Death, Fire
Wield Position: Either

The Ring of Embers grants its wearer +2 Defense. When a Fire Mage has this ring, the ring also grants +3 Mana, 25 percent resistance against Water magic, and 10 percent resistance to all other magic. A unit that attacks a Fire Mage wearing this ring runs the risk of being Scalded, losing one Hit Point every two seconds for ten seconds.

LIFE ARTIFACTS

AMULET OF REVELATION

Allowed Classes: Thief
Allowed Faiths: All
Wield Position: Either

The Amulet of Revelation provides its wielder with +2 Armor, +2 Movement, +2 Sight Radius, and the ability to cast the Life spell Detect Death. In addition, the Amulet restores its wearer to full health at the end of every battle.

CHALICE OF LIFE

Allowed Classes: All
Allowed Faiths: Life, Order, Water
Wield Position: Either

The Chalice of Life grants its holder +3 Wisdom, 20 percent resistance to Death magic, and the ability to cast Bless. In addition, the chalice gives a bonus to ale production.

ELVEN CHAIN MAIL

Allowed Classes: Warrior
Allowed Faiths: Life, Water
Wield Position: Left

Elven Chain Mail grants its wielder +3 Defense, +1 fame per day, 30 percent resistance to Death magic, and 10 percent resistance to all other magic. If a Life Warrior who wears Elven Chain Mail drops to five or fewer Hit Points in combat, he will be teleported to a random location on the battle map.

HEALTHBRINGER

Allowed Classes: Mage
Allowed Faiths: All
Wield Position: Right

Healthbringer grants its wielder +1 Defense and increases the wielder's rate of healing by two.

PEACEMAKER

Allowed Classes: Warrior, Mage
Allowed Faiths: Life
Wield Position: Right

Peacemaker provides its holder with +1 Attack and +1 Defense.

RING OF ARCANA

Allowed Classes: Mage
Allowed Faiths: All, Life
Wield Position: Either

The Ring of Arcana grants its wielder 20 percent resistance to Air, Earth, Fire, and Water magic; 30 percent resistance to Chaos, Death, Life, and Order magic; and the ability to cast Dispel Magic. A Life Mage who wears this ring also receives +2 Defense and +3 Wisdom.

RING OF HEALING

Allowed Classes: All
Allowed Faiths: Air, Chaos, Earth, Fire, Life, Order, Water
Wield Position: Either

The Ring of Healing grants its wielder +1 Defense, +10 Hit Points, and the ability to cast the Life spell Heal. In addition, after combat, the wearer of this ring is restored to full health.

RING OF MARKSMANSHIP

Allowed Classes: Thief
Allowed Faiths: All
Wield Position: Either

The Ring of Marksmanship grants its wielder +1 Ranged Attack and +1 Missile Range.

RING OF REDEMPTION

Allowed Classes: Thief
Allowed Faiths: All, Life
Wield Position: Either

The Ring of Redemption grants its wielder +2 Attack, +1 Defense, and +2 Luck. In addition, any enemy struck in combat by the ring's wearer has a chance of falling under the effects of a Confusion spell. A Life Thief who wears this ring also receives +2 Movement.

ORDER ARTIFACTS

AMULET OF CONTROL

Allowed Classes: Mage
Allowed Faiths: All, Order
Wield Position: Either

The Amulet of Control grants its wielder +2 Defense, 20 percent resistance to all magic, and the ability to cast Order's Possession spell. When an Order Mage wears this amulet, resistance to Chaos magic is increased to 30 percent.

AMULET OF DEFENSE

Allowed Classes: All
Allowed Faiths: All
Wield Position: Either

The Amulet of Defense grants its wielder +1 Defense and +1 Stealth.

AMULET OF ORDER

Allowed Classes: All
Allowed Faiths: Life, Order, Water
Wield Position: Either

The Amulet of Order grants its wielder +2 Defense, +2 Strength, and 25 percent resistance to magic. When worn by a worshiper of the Order faith, the amulet also regenerates one Hit Point every seven seconds in combat and restores its holder to full health at the end of combat.

ARMOR OF INSPIRATION

Allowed Classes: Warrior
Allowed Faiths: Death, Earth, Order
Wield Position: Left

Armor of Inspiration provides its wearer with +2 Defense and 20 percent resistance to Chaos magic. When a Warrior of Order wears this armor, the Armor also has a chance of lashing out, dealing damage to enemies who attempt to strike the wearer of this armor.

RING OF CONCENTRATION

Allowed Classes: Thief
Allowed Faiths: All, Order
Wield Position: Either

The Ring of Concentration adds four to the wielder's maximum number of Hit Points, and it grants +2 Sight Radius and +3 Luck. An Order Thief who wears this ring also receives +2 Movement and 500 experience points.

RING OF PROTECTION

Allowed Classes: All
Allowed Faiths: All
Wield Position: Either

The Ring of Protection grants its wielder +1 Defense and +1 Movement.

SHIELD OF RIGHTEOUSNESS

Allowed Classes: Warrior
Allowed Faiths: Chaos, Death, Order, Water
Wield Position: Either

The Shield of Righteousness grants its wielder +1 Defense and the ability to cast the Order spell Leadership. When held by a Warrior of the Order faith, the shield also provides its bearer with 500 experience points.

STAFF OF ENLIGHTENMENT

Allowed Classes: Mage
Allowed Faiths: Air, Life, Order
Wield Position: Right

The Staff of Enlightenment grants its wielder +2 Defense, 1,000 in experience, and the ability to cast the Air spell Guardian Winds.

SWORD OF QUALITY

Allowed Classes: Warrior
Allowed Faiths: Order
Wield Position: Either

The Sword of Quality grants its wielder +1 Attack and +1 Sight Radius.

WATER ARTIFACTS

AMULET OF PERSUASION

Allowed Classes: Thief
Allowed Faiths: All
Wield Position: Either

The Amulet of Persuasion grants its wielder +2 Dexterity, +2 Movement, +2 Stealth, and 250 experience points.

AQUARING

Allowed Classes: Thief
Allowed Faiths: All
Wield Position: Either

The Aquaring grants its wielder +1 Defense and +1 Missile Range.

CORAL SHIELD

Allowed Classes: Warrior
Allowed Faiths: Chaos, Death, Order, Water
Wield Position: Left

The Coral Shield grants its wielder +2 Defense, +2 Strength, 40 percent resistance against Fire magic, and 30 percent resistance against all other magic. When born by a Water Warrior, the shield grants an additional +1 for Defense.

RING OF THE ELEMENTS

Allowed Classes: Mage
Allowed Faiths: All, Water
Wield Position: Either

The Ring of the Elements grants its wielder +2 Defense; +3 Mana; and 30 percent resistance to Air, Earth, Fire, and Water magic. When a Water Mage wears this ring, the resistance to elemental magic is increased to 40 percent.

RING OF SHELTER

Allowed Classes: Thief
Allowed Faiths: Life, Order, Water
Wield Position: Either

The Ring of Shelter grants its wearer +2 Defense, 30 percent resistance against Fire magic, and the ability to cast Water's Steam Cloud spell.

SHARKTOOTH

Allowed Classes: All
Allowed Faiths: Water
Wield Position: Either

Sharktooth grants its wielder +2 Strength, 1,000 experience points, and the ability to cast the Water spell Quick Silver. Additionally, Sharktooth heals its wielder of one Hit Point of damage every three seconds during combat and restores him to full Hit Points at the end of combat.

WATERSTAFF

Allowed Classes: Mage
Allowed Faiths: All
Wield Position: Right

The Waterstaff grants its wielder +1 Defense and +2 Mana.

POTIONS

POTION OF HEALING

Allowed Classes: All
Allowed Faiths: All
Wield Position: Either

By quaffing the Potion of Healing, the drinker can regain a number of Hit Points equal to the number of crystals that were used in the potion's creation.

POTION OF MANA

Allowed Classes: All
Allowed Faiths: All
Wield Position: Either

By quaffing the Potion of Mana, the drinker can regain an amount of Mana equal to the number of crystals that were used in the creation of the potion.

USAGE CHARTS

The following charts show you which artifacts can be used by which faiths and classes. Artifacts in bold type are *Greater Artifacts*. Italics indicate that Champions of the italicized faith can use that particular artifact, but not at its full potential.

The letter in parenthesis after each artifact indicates that item's primary faith (i.e., which faith it belongs to).

> **Italics in the following tables mean the opposite of what they meant in the artifact descriptions. Specifically, italics in the artifact descriptions indicated the faith that got the most out of a given artifact. Italics in these tables signify the faiths that receive less than the artifact's maximum value.**

TABLE 8-1. ARTIFACTS USABLE BY ALL FAITHS.

Thief	Warrior	Mage
Amulet of Defense (O)	Amulet of Defense (O)	Amulet of Chance (C)
Amulet of Persuasion (W)	Luckstone (E)	Amulet of Defense (O)
Amulet of Revelation (L)	Potion of Healing (P)	Cloudstaff (A)
Aquaring (W)	Potion of Mana (P)	Flameshaft (F)
Faerie Ring (A)	Ring of Marksmanship (L)	Goldenrod (E)
Flint Rint (F)	Ring of Protection (O)	Healthbringer (L)
Luckstone (E)		Luckstone (E)
Potion of Healing (P)		Potion of Healing (P)
Potion of Mana (P)		Potion of Mana (P)
Ring of Entanglement (E)		Ring of Anything (C)
Ring of Marksmanship (L)		Ring of Marksmanship (L)
Ring of Mazes (C)		Ring of Protection (O)
Ring of Protection (O)		Shadowstaff (D)
Ring of Stealth (C)		Waterstaff (W)

TABLE 8-2. ARTIFACTS USABLE BY AIR.

Thief	Warrior	Mage
Amulet of Fate (C)	Amulet of Indecision (C)	Amulet of Control (O)
Amulet of Indecision (C)	Burning Blade (F)	Amulet of Indecision (C)
Amulet of Poison (D)	Crystal Ring (E)	Eyes of the Hawk (A)
Aramoug's Amulet (A)	Dragonscale Armor (F)	Gorgon's Staff (E)
Borchert's Torch (F)	Eyes of the Hawk (A)	Kapelke's Ring (A)
Bow of Bakal (L)	Feather Chain Mail (A)	Polymorph Staff (C)
Bow of Balladrine (E)	Kapelke's Ring (A)	Resurrection Staff (L)
Bow of Quaal (A)	Ring of Healing (L)	Ring of Arcana (L)
Kapelke's Ring (A)	Rocca's Chalice (C)	Ring of Azz'taruth (D)
Pixie Dust (A)	Stormbreaker (A)	Ring of the Elements (W)
Reed Bow (E)	Sword of Flames (F)	Ring of the Four Winds (A)
Ring of Concentration (O)	Thunderblade (A)	Ring of Healing (L)
Ring of Healing (L)		Rocca's Chalice (C)
Ring of Redemption (L)		Staff of Animation (D)
Rocca's Chalice (C)		Staff of Asphyxiation (A)
		Staff of Drowning (W)
		Staff of Enlightenment (O)
		Staff of Incineration (F)
		Stone Ring (E)

TABLE 8-3. ARTIFACTS USABLE BY CHAOS.

Thief	Warrior	Mage
Amulet of Fate (C)	Amulet of Illusion (C)	Amulet of Control (O)
Amulet of Illusion (C)	Amulet of Indecision (C)	Amulet of Illusion (C)
Amulet of Indecision (C)	Axe of Chaos (C)	Amulet of Indecision (C)
Amulet of Poison (D)	Axe of Mauling (E)	Gorgon's Staff (E)
Aramoug's Amulet (A)	Coral Shield (W)	Lich Cloak (D)
Borchert's Torch (F)	Crystal Ring (E)	Polymorph Staff (C)
Chakram of Entropy (C)	Great Axe (C)	Resurrection Staff (L)
Pixie Dust (A)	Helm of Asymmetry (C)	Ring of Arcana (L)
Ring of Concentration (O)	Ring of Healing (L)	Ring of Azz'taruth (D)
Ring of Healing (L)	Rocca's Chalice (C)	Ring of the Elements (W)
Ring of Redemption (L)	Shield of Righteousness (O)	Ring of Embers (F)
Rocca's Chalice (C)	Swift Axe (E)	Ring of the Four Winds (A)
		Ring of Healing (L)
		Rocca's Chalice (C)
		Staff of Animation (D)
		Staff of Asphyxiation (A)
		Staff of Drowning (W)
		Staff of Incineration (F)
		Stone Ring (E)

TABLE 8-4. ARTIFACTS USABLE BY DEATH.

Thief	Warrior	Mage
Amulet of Fate (C)	Amulet of Indecision (C)	Amulet of Control (O)
Amulet of Indecision (C)	Armor of Inspiration (O)	Amulet of Indecision (C)
Amulet of Poison (D)	Ashes of Infestation (D)	Ashes of Infestation (D)
Aramoug's Amulet (A)	Coral Shield (W)	Balkoth's Scythe (D)
Ashes of Infestation (D)	Crystal Ring (E)	Gorgon's Staff (E)
Borchert's Torch (F)	Darkblade (D)	Lich Cloak (D)
Death Dagger (D)	Ebony Plate of the Void (D)	Polymorph Staff (C)
Life Stealing Blade (D)	Guardian (O)	Resurrection Staff (L)
Ring of Concentration (O)	Ice Sword (A)	Ring of Arcana (L)
Ring of Leeches (D)	Obsidian Plate (E)	Ring of Azz'taruth (D)
Ring of Redemption (L)	Ring of Leeches (D)	Ring of the Elements (W)
Rocca's Chalice (C)	Rocca's Chalice (C)	Ring of Embers (F)
	Shield of Righteousness (O)	Ring of the Four Winds (A)
	Soul Stealer (D)	Ring of Leeches (D)
	Tidalblade (W)	Rocca's Chalice (C)
		Staff of Animation (D)
		Staff of Asphyxiation (A)
		Staff of Drowning (W)
		Staff of Incineration (F)
		Stone Ring (E)

TABLE 8-5. ARTIFACTS USABLE BY EARTH.

Thief	Warrior	Mage
Amulet of Fate (C)	Amulet of Indecision (C)	Amulet of Control (O)
Amulet of Indecision (C)	Armor of Inspiration (O)	Amulet of Indecision (C)
Amulet of Poison (D)	Axe of Chaos (C)	Crystalmight (E)
Aramoug's Amulet (A)	Axe of Mauling (E)	Gorgon's Staff (E)
Borchert's Torch (F)	Crystal Ring (E)	Lich Cloak (D)
Bow of Bakal (L)	Ebony Plate of the Void (D)	Polymorph Staff (C)
Bow of Balladrine (E)	Great Axe (C)	Resurrection Staff (L)
Reed Bow (E)	Helm of Asymmetry (C)	Ring of Arcana (L)
Ring of Concentration (O)	Obsidian Plate (E)	Ring of Azz'taruth (D)
Ring of Healing (L)	Ring of Healing (L)	Ring of the Elements (W)
Ring of Redemption (L)	Rocca's Chalice (C)	Ring of the Four Winds (A)
Rocca's Chalice (C)	Swift Axe (E)	Ring of Healing (L)
		Rocca's Chalice (C)
		Staff of Animation (D)
		Staff of Asphyxiation (A)
		Staff of Drowning (W)
		Staff of Incineration (F)
		Stone Ring (E)

TABLE 8-6. ARTIFACTS USABLE BY FIRE.

Thief	Warrior	Mage
Amulet of Fate (C)	Amulet of Indecision (C)	Amulet of Control (O)
Amulet of Indecision (C)	Burning Blade (F)	Amulet of Indecision (C)
Amulet of Poison (D)	Crystal Ring (E)	Eternal Flame (F)
Aramoug's Amulet (A)	Dragonscale Armor (F)	Gorgon's Staff (E)
Borchert's Torch (F)	Eternal Flame (F)	Lich Cloak (D)
Crossbow of Balance (O)	Feather Chain Mail (A)	Polymorph Staff (C)
Eternal Flame (F)	Ring of Brimstone (F)	Resurrection Staff (L)
Ring of Brimstone (F)	Ring of the Dancing Flame (F)	Ring of Arcana (L)
Ring of Concentration (O)	Ring of Healing (L)	Ring of Azz'taruth (D)
Ring of the Dancing Flame (F)	Rocca's Chalice (C)	Ring of Brimstone (F)
Ring of Healing (L)	Stormbreaker (A)	Ring of the Dancing Flame (F)
Ring of Redemption (L)	Sword of Flames (F)	Ring of the Elements (W)
Rocca's Chalice (C)	Thunderblade (A)	Ring of Embers (F)
The Spitfire (F)		Ring of the Four Winds (A)
		Ring of Healing (L)
		Rocca's Chalice (C)
		Staff of Animation (D)
		Staff of Asphyxiation (A)
		Staff of Drowning (W)
		Staff of Incineration (F)
		Stone Ring (E)

TABLE 8-7 ARTIFACTS USABLE BY LIFE.

Thief	Warrior	Mage
Amulet of Fate (C)	Amulet of Indecision (C)	Amulet of Control (O)
Amulet of Indecision (C)	Amulet of Order (O)	Amulet of Indecision (C)
Amulet of Order (O)	Chalice of Life (L)	Amulet of Order (O)
Amulet of Poison (D)	Crystal Ring (E)	Chalice of Life (L)
Aramoug's Amulet (A)	Elven Chain Mail (L)	Eyes of the Hawk (A)
Borchert's Torch (F)	Fyes of the Hawk (A)	Gorgon's Staff (E)
Bow of Bakal (L)	Kapelke's Ring (A)	Kapelke's Ring (A)
Bow of Balladrine (E)	Peacemaker (L)	Peacemaker (L)
Bow of Quaal (A)	Ring of Healing (L)	Polymorph Staff (C)
Chalice of Life (L)	Rocca's Chalice (C)	Resurrection Staff (L)
Kapelke's Ring (A)	Staff of Light (L)	Ring of Arcana (L)
Pixie Dust (A)		Ring of Azz'taruth (D)
Reed Bow (E)		Ring of the Elements (W)
Ring of Concentration (O)		Ring of the Four Winds (A)
Ring of Healing (L)		Ring of Healing (L)
Ring of Redemption (L)		Rocca's Chalice (C)
Ring of Shelter (W)		Staff of Animation (D)
Rocca's Chalice (C)		Staff of Asphyxiation (A)
		Staff of Drowning (W)
		Staff of Enlightenment (O)
		Staff of Incineration (F)
		Staff of Light (L)
		Stone Ring (E)

TABLE 8-8. ARTIFACTS USABLE BY ORDER.

Thief	Warrior	Mage
Amulet of Fate (C)	Amulet of Indecision (C)	Amulet of Control (O)
Amulet of Indecision (C)	Amulet of Order (O)	Amulet of Indecision (C)
Amulet of Order (O)	Armor of Inspiration (O)	Amulet of Order (O)
Amulet of Poison (D)	Chalice of Life (L)	Chalice of Life (L)
Aramoug's Amulet (A)	Coral Shield (W)	Eyes of the Hawk (A)
Borchert's Torch (F)	Crystal Ring (E)	Gorgon's Staff (E)
Chalice of Life (L)	Darkblade (D)	Kapelke's Ring (A)
Crossbow of Balance (O)	Ebony Plate of the Void (D)	Polymorph Staff (C)
Kapelke's Ring (A)	Eyes of the Hawk (A)	Resurrection Staff (L)
Ring of Concentration (O)	Guardian (O)	Ring of Arcana (L)
Ring of Healing (L)	Ice Sword (A)	Ring of Azz'taruth (D)
Ring of Productivity (O)	Kapelke's Ring (A)	Ring of the Elements (W)
Ring of Redemption (L)	Obsidian Plate (E)	Ring of the Four Winds (A)
Ring of Shelter (W)	Ring of Healing (L)	Ring of Healing (L)
Rocca's Chalice (C)	Ring of Productivity (O)	Ring of Productivity (O)
The Spitfire (F)	Rocca's Chalice (C)	Rocca's Chalice (C)
	Shield of Righteousness (O)	Staff of Animation (D)
	Soul Stealer (D)	Staff of Asphyxiation (A)
	Sword of Quality (O)	Staff of Drowning (W)
	Tidalblade (W)	Staff of Enlightenment (O)
		Staff of Incineration (F)
		Stone Ring (E)

TABLE 8-9 ARTIFACTS USABLE BY WATER.

Thief	Warrior	Mage
Amulet of Fate (C)	Amulet of Indecision (C)	Amulet of Control (O)
Amulet of Indecision (C)	Amulet of Order (O)	Amulet of Indecision (C)
Amulet of Order (O)	Aramoug's Amulet (A)	Amulet of Order (O)
Amulet of Poison (D)	Chalice of Life (L)	Aramoug's Amulet (A)
Aramoug's Amulet (A)	Coral Shield (W)	Chalice of Life (L)
Blowgun of the Amazons (W)	Crystal Ring (E)	Gorgon's Staff (E)
Borchert's Torch (F)	Darkblade (D)	Polymorph Staff (C)
Chalice of Life (L)	Elven Chain Mail (L)	Resurrection Staff (L)
Ring of Concentration (O)	Guardian (O)	Ring of Arcana (L)
Ring of Healing (L)	Ice Sword (A)	Ring of Azz'taruth (D)
Ring of Redemption (L)	Ring of Healing (L)	Ring of the Elements (W)
Ring of Shelter (W)	Rocca's Chalice (C)	Ring of the Four Winds (A)
Rocca's Chalice (C)	Sharktooth (W)	Ring of Healing (L)
Sharktooth (W)	Shield of Righteousness (O)	Rocca's Chalice (C)
	Soul Stealer (D)	Sharktooth (W)
	Tidalblade (W)	Staff of Animation (D)
		Staff of Asphyxiation (A)
		Staff of Drowning (W)
		Staff of Incineration (F)
		Stone Ring (E)

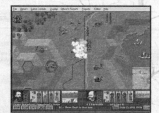   

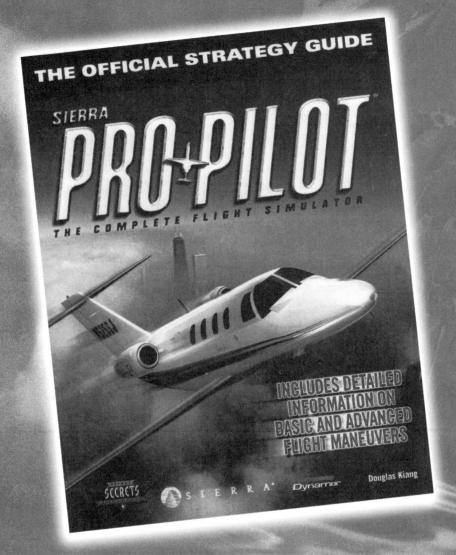